MW00575977

DAVIDIC REFORMATION

Restoring Honor Back to Judah

Apostle Jacques C. Cook

DAVIDIC REFORMATION

Copyright © 2018 by Jacques C. Cook
Published by Reaction Rich Publishing
Benton Harbor, Michigan

Printed in the United States of America
ISBN: 978-0692092989

Library of Congress Cataloging-in-Publication Data

Contents

Foreword   5

Letter from the Author   7

Introduction   9

Chapter One: Davidic Reformation   13

Chapter Two: The Attack Against Judah   35

Chapter Three: The Vehicle to Reform   53

Chapter Four: The Role of Minstrels   65

Chapter Five: The Role of Psalmists   85

Chapter Six: The David/Saul Dynamic   99

Chapter Seven: The Songs of Saul vs. Davidic Songs   107

Chapter Eight: The Forbidden Instrument   115

Chapter Nine: Favorites   123

Chapter Ten: Results of Being Dishonored   139

Chapter Eleven: Solutions for Leaders   149

About the Author   161

DAVIDIC REFORMATION

Foreword

I met Jacques 11 years ago in a prophetic conference in Antioch, California. He had given me a prophetic word that I was an apostle and that I was being given a new seat of authority. And because of this encounter between us, we began to get acquainted over the phone and for all these years since, there has been a lot of ministry exchange between us. Jacques has prophetically ministered to me many times, bringing me much encouragement, and I have ministered to him in discipleship through his many trials and hardships.

Through the ongoing interaction we've had, I have truly had the privilege of getting to know him in a very real, up front and transparent way. And it is because of the consistent character and humility that I saw in him even when I had to bring correction, that I have stood with him all these years even though there were many trying, tumultuous times.

Jacques is one of God's epistles that shall be read of all men, and He is a voice for God who will be heard broadly in our day. It is remarkable to me how thoroughly and deeply God has broken him and now made him so new, just as He wants to do with all His people in order that He can give them a new life in Christ.

When I stayed with Jacques and his family in the Chicago area for the first time in September 2017, I tasted Heaven on Earth. I felt the purity of his/their love and the beauty of who he has become. I later realized that being with Jacques and his family was the "family of God" I was experiencing. It was so special.

Through each trial, God has imparted to Jacques such wisdom and insight that I have cherished every time he shared any of it with me, and I am waiting with bated breath to read this book because I've had a foretaste and I know it will be ALL God and it will be ALL GLORIOUS!

May the Lord be glorified!

-by apostle Dorothy Lee, a Mother in Zion

Letter from the Author

I want to be the first, as an apostolic voice, to repent for the delay in writing this book. Though I have been teaching the revelations in this book for quite some time, I stalled in writing this book, because God wanted me to live it first. This book is not a collection of knowledge. The book shares what I lived and what I am guilty of. I'm guilty by association because I am a part of the Body of Christ. The Body is in ruins and it starts with the arts. This is a part of reform and reconciliation. I'm sharing how dishonor can cause disease and how the systems of Saul produce nothing but premature death and destruction.

I, myself, was almost a casualty of the system of Saul. The only thing that saved me from dying prematurely and being destroyed was I followed the Word that shows where David got everything that was on Saul's life and everything God promised for his life because he didn't retaliate. Needless to say, I didn't retaliate and I'm not going to. From this day forward I will contend for the glory.

All my life I've struggled with my true identity. As a result of struggling with our identity, we generally try to prove who we are or that we are not who people say we are. Since God has delivered me, I've accepted that I am who He made me to be. I now know I don't have to prove; I just need to be.

Apostle Jacques C. Cook, Original

DAVIDIC REFORMATION

Introduction

My goal is to share what the Father has taught me, shown me, as well as what I've experienced in the Body of Christ. As an apostle, I am tasked with bringing order to the divine arts in the area of Davidic reformation. The purpose of this book is to restore order, but you will also find that at times I leave you with questions. Though you will find answers here, my assignment is not to answer everything specific to your situation. My assignment is to bring an awareness concerning some of the misalignment we're experiencing in the Body of Christ across the board-in Judah and other ministry gifts. As an apostle, I realize that all churches are not the same, and you have to deal with it on a case by case scenario. It's best to seek God, and do what's best for your house. So you may ask, "What do I do with the questions I am left with?" Ask the Father to help you move into reformation and if need be, ask Him to guide you to a specialist in this area. People, like myself, can come in and help set order. We seek out specialists in every other area of life. I've found that the divine arts are the most used function in the Body of Christ, but the most neglected. Often times we tend to put more money behind flesh than we do the spiritual things that will benefit us. Sadly, what's sacred to God, is not sacred to us. If I could give you all the answers in this book, it would handicap you from seeking out the answers. God desires to give you answers to your specific situation and send you the help you need. My assignment is to restore purity and clarity, which will eventually restore the state of divine arts in the Body of Christ.

The Ministry of Divine Arts is in ruin, as much as the twin towers were on 9/11. We have more fan-fair today than effectiveness. It has to stop and we have to restore order. We want divas instead of ministers. Instead of us correcting it, we're building on top of a weak foundation. We build on top of our iniquity. We sweep our mess under the rugs, instead of pulling the rug and dealing with it. We are afraid to risk our accountability with people, so we ignore it. Yet, we'll risk our accountability with God.

I understand that I will get some challenge on the correction that comes with restoring order. I also understand that my motives will be questioned about writing this book. I do not write because I am a subject matter expert. I know what I know because I've lived what I write. This is what makes it credible. It's my life experience.

Finally, in the book of Judges, we see two instances where God commissioned the tribe of Judah to go up first against their enemies in battle before the rest of the army. God set up the battle to be won through the release of the tactic of praise, first. When the tribe of Judah offered praise at the beginning of the battle, the victory was won. If the Bible clearly acknowledges that Judah had to go first before all battles, are we not to continue operating in the same function? Are we not in a major battle in the Body right now? Judah must still go first. However, to do so, Judah needs to be cleaned up. We need to be set back in order to be effective. We are unclean. We are listening to music that no longer brings honor to God. Our praise and worship is structured to only sing songs we want to hear, with no regard for what God wants. We are no longer on the same frequency with God. We've stopped asking what is going on in Heaven. We begin our services playing what we want.

Every time I lead worship, I ask God to let us in wherever Heaven is already flowing. We have to ask for access to align ourselves with the frequency of Heaven. It is time for us to allow reformation to take place in and through us. As we are reformed, the Body will be reformed, and eventually, we can allow reformation to flow to the world. Lord, let this book bring life to me and others, and protect the lives of those whose heart is truly after God. *Amen*

Judah as the tribe of praise?

DAVIDIC REFORMATION

Chapter One
Davidic Reformation

What is Davidic Reformation?

$\mathcal{D}$avidic Reformation is the reformation of Church as we know it, where each five-fold ministry gift functions appropriately. The Body of Christ is currently functioning from an incorrect foundation that was built improperly and duplicated from learned behavior. Since it was built incorrectly in the first place, the Body of Christ can only go so far. The foundation is not deep enough to handle growth.

The object of reform is to point us back to Jesus and bring the heart of God back to the forefront. This should have been our central focus in the first place but has progressively changed. Our focus is more on numbers and pleasing ourselves, as opposed to total obedience to the Word of God. We are losing more people to other Gods than we ever have in history. We've lost our focus.

> "I hate, I despise your feasts, and I take no delight in your solemn assemblies. Even though you offer me your burnt offerings and grain offerings, I will not accept them; and the peace offerings of your fattened animals, I will not look upon them. Take away from me the noise of your songs; to the melody of your harps I will not listen. But let justice roll down like waters, and righteousness like an ever-flowing stream. Amos 5:21-24

There are many areas in which we, as the Body of Christ, need reform. This passage truly conveys the heart of God concerning our refusal to realign. God will hate, despise, and take no delight in what we offer Him. Imagine our most enthusiastic services where we've offered the best songs, the most impressive prayers, and the fieriest sermons. When righteousness [holiness, blamelessness] and justice [integrity, honesty, uprightness] does not govern us, Scripture witnesses that God says He will *not* listen to those very things we work so hard to offer. Is not our worship meant to solely please and honor Him? The reality is that we're offering God programs, but He wants relationship. We sing, "*We bring the sacrifice of praise into the house of the Lord...and we offer unto you the sacrifices of thanksgiving...*" In this new covenant, He wants _you_ as a sacrifice; not sacrifice. We have been offering up what we choose to offer up, not what He requires. This is why reform is necessary right now. The offerings mentioned above are exactly what Saul did. God told Saul to kill everything when he went into the camp of the Amalekites, but Saul disobeyed and saved God something (I Samuel 15). God never instructed Saul to save what he should've killed and offer it as a sacrifice (vs. 15). The greatest sacrifice Saul could have offered God was the simple obedience of killing every enemy of God in that camp. And in many ways, here is the picture of the Body of Christ, today. Instead of us killing _everything_ that God instructed us to kill, and not save it for ourselves, we hold something back and offer it as a sacrifice. God is not pleased with the sacrifice rooted in disobedience. Instead of dismantling shaky foundations and ungodly systems and rebuilding on obedience, we hold some of the "choicest" traditions back and add them upon the incorrect foundation.

To rebuild, we have to begin with Judah (The Ministry of the Arts). In the Old Testament, worshiping God was the first thing required to precede any battle, and is the only thing we are going to be doing for eternity. Davidic reformation is the process that will set us on the right foundation and point us back to God's desired design for the Body of Christ. There are too many deaths, too much sickness, and too many repercussions for us not to yield to reform. We desperately need God to hear us, again. The formula given to us to ensure this begins at obeying God's instructions.

> If my own people will humbly pray and turn back to me and stop sinning, then I will answer them from Heaven. I will forgive them and make their land fertile once again. I will hear the prayers made in this temple, because it belongs to me, and this is where I will be worshiped forever. I will never stop watching over it (2 Chronicles 7:14-16 CEB).

My Reformation Journey

My parents were in ministry, pastoring, and got tired of looking for musicians, as they struggled to keep one. My mother prayed that a musician would come through her womb. I was born and began to play at age six, with no lessons and no sight-reading lessons, either. Every time I tried to sight read, it wouldn't work. As I got older, I played for my dad. We were so close in the context of ministry that my dad would be thinking of a song, I would start playing, then my mom would sing it. As early as the late 70's, in my adolescence, I was flowing prophetically and didn't know what it was. When we sang songs in my dad's church, they were songs we wrote. We didn't know they were songs of the Lord; we were just flowing. I was being trained as a minstrel in the 1970s.

In high school band competitions, we were told if we couldn't sight read, we need to leave. My mom begged them to give me a chance by allowing me to hear the song and then allowing me to play it. They played it one time and I got on the keyboard and played it, note for note. They then sent home the other six people auditioning. I played for that school for six years, although I only went to the school for one year. After graduating, they made me shave my beard, to play for them.

Everything I was told I couldn't do, I did. In high school talent shows, I was the only one that people listened to. I DJ'd- making house music and was the first DJ to mix rap music. After high school, I went into the secular music industry where I recorded for secular artists. I worked in the studio with some of the largest artists. I was sent overseas, working with people like Toni Braxton, Donna Summers, Faith Evans, R. Kelly, and more. This educated me on different technologies of recording. I was writing songs and had never been taught how. While in that arena I got caught up in a backslidden state of mind and while in that state of mind, my roots were the supernatural. So I learned what it is to have a form of Godliness but deny the power thereof. I only wanted to make money. Then I got into drugs. They paid me in drugs, instead of money. Well-known music producers never paid me. They cheated me out of commercial royalties for my music that traveled overseas. I didn't know anything about business matters and made so many mistakes. This is why I have such a heart to help artists understand the business of the industry and how to protect themselves.

I was always different. I came to church to play after being a DJ overnight. Being a DJ, I learned that when you're talented, you can move the crowd. I learned to keep a constant flow, so the owner could sell liquor. I had a gift, I knew how to keep a flow. When the owner said he needed to sell beer, I put on house music. When he wanted to sell wine, I put on male singers to seduce women. When he needed to sell brown hard liquor, I put on blues to get people vexed to drink liquor. This is the exact example of what manipulation looks like. In the church, preachers say, "play some giving music." That's manipulation. Today, I will not allow you to use me to play something to get money out of people. I refuse; because this is the manipulation I participated in, in the world. When I was younger, I even allowed my father to use me to play something "to get the people to give." This is why leaders should not be guiding minstrels to hear from Holy Spirit. They can set you up to be in error. And this is the picture of our churches today. Our churches look like talk shows. Our instruments are set up at the corner of the stage. The stage is reserved for celebrities that help people to give. Our churches are a show.

Growing older, as an adult, I still played in the club on Friday and Saturday night. The same band that

played for me at the club, played for the choir. When
we opened our cases, smoke came out from the club we
played in the night before. I know it goes on because I
did it. I lived so dangerously. I was getting high and
having sex with the singers and the preacher's
daughter. I was sleeping with girls in the choir and
taking communion. I was partaking of the Lord's body
but had no fear of taking it unworthily. Even in all this, I
still had a hunger for God, as my purpose for being here
was greater than my appetite for sin. I was in a
backslidden state. My sister prayed me back. When you
have been prayed into the Earth, you can't get away
from it. The prayer over my life was that I would be
sent to this Earth to bring purity and accuracy.

After returning from a life of sin in my backslidden
state, the first church I went to had an excellent music
ministry, but no anointing. From day one, my spirit
man was crying out for more. It knew that environment
wasn't it when I didn't. After being there for several
years, I decided to get saved. Let me say this, when I got
saved, things didn't get rosy. That's when all of my
problems began. When I got saved and Holy Spirit
filled, my band kicked me out. I constantly relived the
David/Saul dynamic. Growing up in a church where I
was a PK (preacher's kid), I found myself involved in
that relationship dynamic with not only my biological
father but other pastors and leaders that did not know
how to father the uniqueness in me. They tried to
conform me into a musician and singer, but God called

me to be a psalmist and a minstrel. I needed to be delivered from the soul-tie between me and my father. I later found out that he was a musician and didn't want to tell us. He spoke word curses over my music, as he was more interested in using my music for *his* purposes. Most places I've cast my lot, the David/Saul dynamic presented itself. I didn't understand it, or why most leaders I've come into contact with want me to just shut up and play. They were not interested in the other dimensions of my life beyond the keyboard. So, I have been like this all of my life. The warfare began and things got worse. I began to experience warfare, betrayal, and abuse on a level that I couldn't imagine would ever happen.

Throughout my entire life, it has been difficult for me to learn and remember songs that are scripted. It has caused me to have a false reproach on my name that I don't work well with others. Things I share with people from the Lord, people receive it as if I am nuts. You have to be careful when people speak well over you, as it's often a smokescreen for what they actually feel about you. They are often intimidated that you can make decisions on your own. I was marked as a renegade because I had a relationship with God and could hear from him for myself. Saul was jealous and threatened by David because of this same thing. You are a threat to any controlling leader when you exercise having a brain and relationship with God for yourself. They are intimidated by a similar spirit. They

have an inability to honor you but will use you. I found
they use false doctrine to control you. As a result of this
happening in my life, I spent years walking in a false
humility, when it was actually stupidity.

My ability to access realms and set an atmosphere
was the only thing that seemed to draw interest to
myself. I served under leaders that didn't care about
me as a person. There was no honor from the church to
support my music. I had to supplement life by making a
living outside of the church. Walking in dishonor
opened me up to disease. I contracted a disease called
diabetes, which God later healed me from. I took a
biblical approach of, "God forgive them for they know
not what they do." As David received what Saul did not
because he didn't retaliate, I am attempting to mirror
my life with the same heart. I have no desire to retaliate
against leaders that were acting in ignorance.
Therefore, I am sharing my situation in hopes to help
leaders who have experienced similar. I will not cover
wrong motives or wrongdoings. I feel we've done this
far too long because the church is afraid to face truth.
This needs to be faced now because increasingly,
people are dying far before their time. Five or more
musicians I know died before their time, because of a
broken heart. They served faithfully alongside leaders
and administrators, expecting to be honored, but
instead were sent out to supplement their lives with
other jobs. I know of others who were broken from
being overlooked because they didn't have what the

church wanted (although they had what God wanted). The blood is on our hands as we refuse to change or take responsibility for dishonoring and causing early death in people, from broken hearts. This has to change.

As my journey continued, I served as a minstrel, in several different churches and organizations. I discovered I was more than a keyboardist. I discovered I was a ministry gift. I created my own itinerary. It caused me to follow a pattern that wasn't for me. I got caught up thinking the apostolic was something I saw others do. When I searched Ephesians' teaching about Christ giving gifts, I realized there was a reason that it mentions "he gave some apostles," first. When I asked the Lord what was my assignment and my original purpose for coming to the Earth, He told me I was sent to bring clarity and purity to the arts and all the functions adjacent to it (especially praise and worship and minstrel functions). I also discovered I had to live out these functions, instead of merely sharing information. I had to become the revelation to me first. I was ordained a prophet at the age of nine, but I discovered the apostolic later in my life. When I traveled in ministry, Holy Spirit gave me to release people into their destinies. When God revealed the type of apostle I was (which is an apostle of the divine arts) he showed me how I'd already been doing the work. That's why this book was created- to share my godly experiences to solidify the revelation I'm sharing.

Hence, the mentioning of apostles first, in Ephesians 4 is because we are called to step in *first* and be the *first* to experience. Because of the revelation and understanding the Father released to me, I often clash with leaders who are insecure with who they are, or are selfish and want to shine before a crowd instead of being a team-player. I set standards in my life that line up with the Word of God. I wouldn't allow them to use me to fleece the crowd or to misuse me to line up with their agendas.

I am in the season of recovery from being dishonored by people for over 20 plus years of my life. As a result of dishonor, my kidneys shut down. I lost my sight, where I could not drive anywhere. Yet, God has restored those areas. God exposed to me that I was not at the level I thought I was. As a result, it's made me redefine what worship really is and, in turn, go deeper with God. Looking back, I was acquainted with God through religion, but I didn't really know Him. Truth be told, God didn't download anything new in me. It was already in me; I just didn't access it. The land that God showed Abraham didn't just appear, it was already there; he just couldn't see it. Abraham had to submit to being led to it. This came from an activation of trust. I've found that it's easy for us to believe God, but we struggle to trust Him. When you believe in somebody, if they do something contrary to what you think they should do, your belief is tested. On the contrary, when you trust them, you don't care what they do. I've always believed that God heals, but at times when I woke up and didn't have my sight restored, I started questioning Him. That's a sign that I didn't trust Him. So, after venting and asking for clarity, I yielded to trusting. I have been saying for years that I believe, but I *MUST* trust Him. That's not easy, but when my sight is blurry, my gratefulness that I can see causes me to trust Him.

I thank God for opening my eyes and shielding me from the bitterness of the systems that refuse to change. I don't get upset with the systems, I get upset with the spirits behind them. I ask God to raise my love level for people and my hate level for the systems that are contrary to His system. It burdens me to see people flock to these systems because they appear to be what the majority are embracing. Realistically, we are conditioned to flock toward the majority, but that that represents the minority is never popular. By default, people tend to embrace things that don't provoke them to go higher because it's not a challenge. We've conditioned people to fear freedom. In any other system, we hate to be controlled. Yet, when we get in the Kingdom of God and taste freedom, we are upset because no one is controlling us. What needs to be dealt with and abolished is this slave mentality. Because of this existing ungodly system, we don't even know how to be free. I've seen slave mentality right in the church. People have been conditioned to serve a leader and be faithful to them for years before the leader will promote them. This is ungodly. Biblically, a leader is supposed to serve and promote others. We've got it so backward that things like this become our governing statutes and are handed off from generation to generation as "*the* way."

Now, a brief disclaimer: I am prepared for the onslaught of leaders that will challenge all I'm saying out of a place of guilt. I do not present truth to attack you. I present truth to set the Body of Christ free and expose the ungodly cycles we've perpetuated that produce ungodly fruit. Truth needs no rebuttal. The truth of God stands alone.

As a result of standing on and speaking up for righteousness and truth, I have had leaders move to shut me up and tell me to simply play the keyboard. They don't want me to share truth. They only want me to play and sing. The reason I cannot do that is I am not only a worship leader, singer, or instrument; I am a ministry gift. I was sent to the Earth to bring clarity to the misuse of ministry gifts. Ministry gifts are not limited to gifts and talents; people are ministry gifts, as well. Therefore, I am sent to bring clarity to the misuse of people and the gifts and talents they've been equipped with. I am never surprised when I'm slighted. I'm never surprised when I am invited somewhere and share what's in me, that I'm never invited back again. I was not sent to take engagements. I was sent to release truth and take divine assignments. I was designed by God. I was sent by God. My assignment is to God. My motto is, "If God ain't sayin' it, I ain't doin' it."

Essentially, I've allowed God to anoint the character He put in me. That is a no-nonsense character that speaks up and tells the truth. Even if this truth closes the doors that man opened. There are doors that God opens that no man can close. I lived for myself for my first 50 years, but come what may, the rest is for Him.

No More Compromise

As an apostle, I am a wise master-builder and need places where I can pour and build- not create a place to get money out of people. I cannot do that anymore. Half of the engagements that people take are not from God, that's why they get worn out. When your focus is *solely* on engagements and the honorarium that comes with it, the truth is your goal is to supplement the lavish lifestyle you live, instead of pouring into people to help them to create realms that will sustain them for life. David didn't take from people, he poured into them. I have a problem when the set leader lives a life of luxury when 70 percent of the church is on government assistance. I also have a problem when leaders ask people in the arts to serve without compensation when you (as a leader) cannot preach without getting compensation. Then we throw out Scriptures about doing what we do as unto the Lord. If that's the case, so should you. I think leaders should first try to have some sort of income (even a job), instead of living off what is coming from the people through offerings. You should certainly have some type of vocation. The church offering should be something extra. The offerings and tithes are meant to care for those who serve. This is why, if your arts leaders don't work outside of the church, they can't live. Yet, this isn't taking place across the board. The surplus is in the pastor's house. This foolishness is all being exposed now. This is why pastors are being indicted for mishandling of funds. My point is, don't ask someone to do something you are unwilling to do yourself. That makes you a liar and hypocrite. No one wants to deal with that. I would feel some type of way if I gave to a church and when I needed help, the church didn't have it.

The church is not even in a position to meet the needs of those serving in Judah. Religion has programmed us to train shepherds to ask support from the sheep when the shepherd should seek out ways to depend on God to supply what is needed to take care of the sheep. That's if you are truly a shepherd. A father provides for his family. The family doesn't provide for the father. God instituted the family dynamic. "Our Father which art in Heaven..." (Matthew 6:9-13). The function of providing for the set father is off. David not only went to battle, he collected the spoils of war. The set man staying at home while everyone else goes out to war is off. Scripture shows David got in trouble when he did not go out, "At a time when King's go to war..." (2 Samuel 11). We need reform. We have little boys and girls in places of authority. Little boys and girls still want to play. They have no heart to bring order. That's why reform is bringing the heart of God back to the forefront. Today the building of one's own ministry and empire is at the forefront. How many of us have heard leaders say, "How many you runnin', doc?" My response to them is, "How many you runnin' straight to hell?" Their only focus is how many people are paying their 10 percent from week to week. If you were more soul conscious, if one left, you would just go get another one. So essentially, we've fallen short because we provide for the set man or father of the house. Yet, it should be the other way around where the father provides. Sheep don't take care of the shepherd; the shepherd takes care of the sheep.

Getting Judah cleaned up is the start. We need to help the singers make the transition to psalmists, and musicians converting to minstrels. Call a thing according to its functions, not talents. Musicians move the crowd; minstrels move the cloud. In this hour beloved, if you can't demonstrate it you shouldn't teach it. David provided for the needs of everyone- even his enemy. No creature, let alone a talented individual, can access God's glory in a consistent way when they are distracted by bills and cares of this life. David had no lack in his camp because he wasn't selfish. David eliminated all the distractions from the worshiper's life, so they could worship. David bought land for them to inhabit. Part of the lack we see today comes from the

Body of Christ not being on the right frequency in this area.

God used me in different nations to impart the gift to play instruments, supernaturally. The way He gives it to me, I impart it to others. Present day, I am embarking on opening several schools of the arts to train minstrels and psalmists, so they are raised up the Kingdom and Biblical way. The only ability I have is to hear from Holy Spirit. I have not learned from any man. The results I get are out of this world, literally, because I am co-dependent on Holy Spirit. I don't know anything else and don't want to know anything else, as it keeps me from taking credit for what I've invested in myself. Sending psalmists and minstrels to systems that were created by man locks them into a limited parameter where they can only go so far. It's like a cloning process, where you're limited by man. Holy Spirit has no limitations. I have never experienced writer's block. There is no such thing. Holy Spirit doesn't run out of anything- we do. I am still seeking God on how to carry out my original purpose for being sent to the Earth.

Whenever you don't know the true purpose of something (person, place or, thing), you will abuse and mishandle it. I have seen this happen to minstrels and psalmists. Musicians and singers don't have those issues, as they come a dime a dozen. There is no threat to them. There is no challenge for them to live right, either. As leaders, we ought to be ashamed, when we don't challenge people to live right. I've seen it on both sides; being a leader and coming up on the side of a musician. I've played for people secularly and in the church who thought their name was greater than God. They did not want me to obey God. They wanted me to obey them. I've seen more treachery in the church than in the secular arena. The only thing that caused me to survive was that God was killing me so that I wouldn't feel any of it.

The Lord sent me on assignment to the streets of Chicago in vacant lots, where murders took place so that I could play and excavate the soil. He said, "I want you to go and play where no one knows your name or title." God showed me a picture of David playing under the tent where he had 288 singers skilled in the song of the Lord, and 4000 musicians giving praise on instruments he created (I Chronicles 23-25). They were all in one accord and this technology caused everyone to prosper. Sidebar: How can 4288 people get on one accord to the point that it produces Kingdom results, but we can't get seven people on our praise and worship team to get on one accord? Something is wrong. God asked me what was under the tent. I said soil. He said, "David tapped into technology in that day, where he was able to send music into the ground." The ground yielded whatever he needed. The ground yields everything of value we need. David had no lack in his camp. The purpose of David excavating the soil in this manner points to the knowledge that everything we profit from grows from the ground. Gold is mined. Silver is mined. That's why he was able to prosper. The frequencies from the music went into the ground to yield everything David needed to prosper. The pageantry of Heaven is so rich in the display of this technology. What David produced was so rich and prosperous that I've patterned my life after it to yield everything I need. We are made of dirt/soil. When Judah goes forth to worship, they are excavating the soil of individuals who are made from dirt. That's the benefit of having minstrels instead of musicians. This is where leaders have missed it. When you allow minstrels to go forth, you are excavating soil, to allow people to prosper. Unfortunately, we want people who just sing and perform well- when all they do is take away, instead of producing change. This is why it's important for our music ministries to function by biblical structures.

In 1 Chronicles 25:1-6, David identified the fathers and sent the fathers to identify the sons, because they were identified by the strengths they had. Today, natural and spiritual fathers hoard their sons. Fathers want to hold their armies to make themselves look good. Send the armies out! Numerous apostles and pastors, today, don't know what they're doing. On one end, we see apostles who possess the title but have a pastoral grace. Yet, on the other end we have pastors holding their titles, but operating under apostolic grace. Both are afraid to step into their grace, because of what other people may say. There are enough people in the world for apostles to take their place. It is badly needed in Judah. Where are the apostles to release this band of warriors we saw in I Chronicles? They don't operate with normalcy. This band of warriors doesn't even know what normal is. They need a father to release and speak over them, so they can be fruitful. They don't need to be shut down, only to be released when their leader is too old to serve. Those days are over.

Where Do We Begin?

The purpose of this book is to help churches, nations, and people get free from religious foolishness. I'm tired of hearing and seeing the effects of the same ungodly spirits running rampant in the Body. People can't get to God because of their experience with little boys in the pulpit and the church hurt they carry from 27 years ago.

We perpetuate behaviors and refuse to question rituals in our churches that are unbiblical. Have you ever wondered why we (as the church) adopt trends that acclimate us to the trends of the world? Why do we turn the lights off during worship, like we are in a club? If we can't connect and apprehend God with the lights on, we will fail with the lights off. Intimacy in our personal relationship is the missing ingredient. We are not wooing the Godhead, we're wooing ourselves.

Sin and ungodliness are overlooked depending on how much money a person has. Status has replaced standards. Money has replaced morals. Our stages have become a place where if the congregation is not impressed, there's no demand placed on the atmosphere to produce. We've grown motivated by being impressed, more than being ministered to. Where do we begin?

DAVIDIC REFORMATION

Chapter Two
The Attack Against Judah

Who is Judah?

Jacob had 12 sons, and Judah was the fourth child born to him and Leah. The name Judah means "Praise." Yet, Judah's name is associated more with sound rather than singing. Out of Jacob's 12 sons, Judah was usually the one that led them into battle (Judges 1:2, 20:18). All of Jacob's sons possessed a sound that they often released in battle, but Judah's sound was different from the rest. When Judah shouted, his voice sounded like a lion's roar and his enemies would lose heart from fear of that sound. Judah and his brothers were some of the fiercest warriors in the Earth. They had a reputation for destroying entire cities with their small army, which caused them to be feared throughout the land.[1] Judah can be described as a mighty warrior, as well as an

ref.

---

[1] Jasher 39:19-21, 30-33, Jasher 54:43-46

??
okay apocrypha.ish.

35

apostle of sound because he was usually sent first. The most important part of Judah's life was affirmed by his father's prophetic impartation.

He said:

> "Judah, your brothers will praise you. You will defeat your enemies. All your relatives will bow before you. Judah is a young lion that has finished eating its prey. Like a lion he crouches and lies down; like a lioness- who will dare to rouse him? The scepter will not depart from Judah, nor the ruler's staff from his descendants, until the coming of the one to whom it belongs, the one whom all nations will obey. He ties his foal to a grapevine, the colt of his donkey to a choice vine. He washes his clothes in wine because his harvest is so plentiful. His eyes are darker than wine, and his teeth are whiter than milk" (Genesis 49:8-12 NLT).

According to tradition, the firstborn child is to receive the greatest honor and blessing. Reuben was the firstborn but his reckless behavior of sleeping with one of his father's wives caused him to be disqualified. The Lord replaced him by making choice of Judah, and his royal lineage became heir to the throne of Israel; the same throne that King David was chosen to rule upon. The coming of the Messiah was also foretold in Judah's prophecy that He would be the final heir to the throne. Releasing a sound that terrifies the enemy was a defining characteristic of the line of Judah. David inherited the pioneering ability in sound and warlike qualities from Judah, and Jesus was proclaimed as "The Lion of the Tribe of Judah." His very presence and purpose terrified the enemy.

Today, Judah is often referred to as those in the Ministry of the Arts. However, Judah does not only represent those who are musically inclined. Judah represents those who have been anointed with the mantel to break barriers, dismantle ungodly systems, and establish the Kingdom of God, using sound. The Ministry of the Arts has carried the anointing to interpret and release prophetic sounds. However, Holy Spirit can also use a corporate and unified Body of believers who surrender to the Davidic call.

Our Present Condition

The scheme of contention that grew between David and Saul is alive and well in the Body of Christ, today. David represented obedience. Saul represented compromise and disobedience. The Body of Christ is in a severe state of compromise. We adopt things that we know aren't godly, but we do it anyway. We don't ask the questions about why they are permitted. Our churches look like a scene from Showtime at the Apollo. If someone doesn't soothe our flesh, we will boo them off the stage. If you don't come with the raw anointing, most won't recognize. We confuse what sounds good with what's anointed, but they are two totally different things. Leaders, when you put energy and money in who can play the most chords, who is the most popular or sought after, who has the best chops, and/or who they are playing with, you are a Saul. David looked at the heart of a man to get an understanding of his intentions. David followed God's instructions to eliminate distractions out of the lives of the people, so they could serve. When we look at the Word where the minstrel was described, they were noted as skillful [qualified, proficient, gifted, adept, dexterous, competent] and cunning [crafty, artful, designing, clever] (I Chronicles 25:7). That has nothing to do with talent alone. The skill reference did not mean the minstrel was talented and knew how to play the best in the land, it meant he had the ability to lead and follow Holy Spirit at the same time. There was an element in David's DNA that gave him the ability to play the evil spirit out of Saul. In fact, the evil spirit was put into Saul by God to create a situation to use a specific someone (who was after God's own heart) to get it out. God could've used any musician, but He chose to use a minstrel. Musicians today come a dime a dozen, but a minstrel is rare. God uses minstrels because of their pursuit of His heart through relationship.

Essentially, the Saul system has ruined our churches. It has led us on the path where we've become irrelevant, by becoming relevant to everything. If we look at our praise and worship service, we look more like the world than ourselves. We've created a culture that accommodates a soul saying, "I'm not going to participate if you don't come to my level." The method needs to change, but the message has always been the same. I will never manipulate my worship to achieve the style of music that people like. I will bring the pure sound that comes from God. That's the only thing that will draw people- even our youth. Research frequently presents new techniques to draw our youth, but the only way to reach young people is to be an adult.

Prophets rarely prophesy the Word of the Lord anymore. They prophesy soothing words. I don't believe in a school of the prophets. Schools only clone the teacher. You can't tell me prophets should have restrictions on how God speaks. How do you tell a prophet they can't deal with certain issues? That's all prophets did in the Word. He sent warning through prophets about areas that needed correction. We've created prophets *we* can control, not authentic prophets.

We tend to worry about things that are God's responsibility. It's not our responsibility if people don't come to church or if they leave your church. If that happens, take the responsibility you've been given to evangelize more people into the Kingdom. Do you know how many souls we walk past to do our daily routines? We can't get caught up in hoarding members. They're not yours anyway; they are God's. *Your* responsibility is to evangelize, disciple, equip, develop, and release them to get more people. I believe this for the ministry of Judah, as well. I don't think that minstrels and psalmists sole influence should be limited to Sunday worship services. They are called to influence and release the Kingdom of the Lord throughout the Earth. Personally, I believe Judah should infiltrate the music industry. How else can they take that mountain of influence and establish the Kingdom of God if they don't go get it?

The Fruit of Ungodly Systems

In a later chapter, we'll discuss in greater depth how you will know when you're in a David and Saul dynamic. However, the symptoms are obvious. Saul thought he could keep doing whatever he wanted to David because he was the king. That's the identical depiction of leaders under the influence of this system. They do whatever they want and think it's okay because of who they are. The mentality of a Saulic leader is, "Psalmist, I'm the king and all I need you to do is sing." To the minstrel, they are saying, "I don't care what you say, I just want you to play." I know first-hand that this can be frustrating, but don't fret. When you don't retaliate and continue worshiping while God works in the situation on your behalf, your worship will act as spiritual forensics to expose the fingerprints on the javelin that was thrown at you. I was gifted to play and it shifted atmospheres. I lived with a false reproach on my name because I was told I was a

warlock due to my God-given ability to access realms. *??*
At the time, I didn't know this was being said because
those same people smiled in my face. Know that evil
men and women play a role in pushing you into your
destiny. I lived by this motto with my Judases, "Do what
you do quickly."

People used by the devil are treacherous. They are
people of compromise and are never a threat to the
enemy. That's why they have no trials. If you examine
yourself and find that you have no resistance in your
life, you have no authority. You're not a threat to the
kingdom of darkness. Because you're ineffective, the
enemy doesn't have to come against you. This is why
the Gospel tells us countless times to rejoice when we
are persecuted. Judah, this is the time to rejoice like a
big fool. It's the only way to keep your sanity. The
attack is coming because of the pioneering grace on
your life. You're graced to be a trendsetter and/or a
reformer. If the enemy can destroy your influence
before you accomplish this, reform won't take place. If
Judah is destroyed, how can it go first in battle? The
Saul system is causing things to change so that Judah *Nina*
will get discouraged and leave the faith. They are being
provoked to leave. The enemy needs your ability to
create because he doesn't have any. If he can
discourage you to leave the faith, he can use your
ability, elsewhere. He uses vessels ordained by God. If
he had the power to create on his own, he wouldn't
steal anything. Your praise and worship ministry

should be used as a spiritual air force. This was the intended purpose for Judah. If you know anything about going to battle, sending Judah first was to clear the airways so the troops didn't get killed. When your praise and worship is out of whack, they aren't clearing airways, so ground troops are getting killed. The battle is with the prince of the power of the air (Ephesians 2:2). I'm asking Judah to have an open mind about who you are. Don't compromise because the enemy wants you to think you have to go to him to get what you need to be effective. How can you go to him for what already belongs to God? The Father already owns what you need.

I believe that all five-fold ministry gifts are disgruntled. However, all sides have a responsibility to work together to find a solution for the compromise taking place in the Body of Christ. More importantly, we all have to get on the right frequency- God's frequency.

The Plight of Judah

If you are faced with a situation where you are being attacked and javelins are being thrown at you, you are familiar with the plight of Judah. David was the perfect example of what to do in this situation. He caught Saul at a disadvantage several times and could've retaliated against him, but he didn't. David ran. No matter what you do, there is no right or wrong way to run. That's religion that says that there is a right and wrong way to leave a church, despite the abuse you're suffering. If someone is attacking, you should be running. Who has time to write a letter when someone is throwing javelins at you? We hide behind systems and standards we created that have nothing to do with God. In my own personal testimony, I was told in several cases that I didn't leave right. In all cases, I went to my leader and shared why I was leaving. All but one released me, so I was forced to leave to obey God's voice. I was then blackballed and labeled a "renegade." Those who remained at the church were told not to have anything to do with me because I was "cursed." I was told that my gifts were only operable because of the church I was in and the leadership I was under. My response was that I had those gifts on me when I was in the streets with a blunt in my mouth. The gifts don't come from the leader or the church but from God. The Saul system always wants to take credit for what you bring to the table. It's notorious for making you feel like you need another person to operate.

So what am I saying? Get out of the Saulic system, because it's never going to change. The only people who will disagree with everything I'm saying in this book are the people guilty of operating in the things I'm exposing. Why else would you disagree with something that brings freedom? This points back to my earlier statement that the Saul system is always rooted in disagreeing with doing what God tells you to do. In the same manner, Saul altered *his* instructions from God to cater to his preference (I Samuel 15). Present day, if God tells us to kill some of the relationships and systems in our life and not spare it, He means just that. When we hold onto them, out of disobedience, we are no better than Saul. In fact, we reap the fruit of Saul's disobedience.

The danger I see in the Saul system, present day, is the collateral damage of death. Saul has been successfully carrying out the assignment to kill the David in you. If that spirit can't physically kill you, it will kill your influence. Obviously, this spirit and system can only stop you if you allow it, but it *can* cause delay. You'll be forced to wait for God to vindicate you, work some things out to preserve your life, and keep you healed. He *will* vindicate and restore honor back to you, but there is a purpose for Him allowing you to go through that process. The purpose is that your eyes will be opened to see that what you carry is valuable to God. You're not obligated to keep releasing what you carry to people who don't appreciate it. You are obligated to God, not man. We have to realize that we are equipped with gifts, but *we* are also the gift that God sends. People are never going to value us when we don't value ourselves. When we make the choice to remain in a system that's killing us, we alone are at fault. The fault does not belong to the person or system that's killing you. Value yourself enough to disallow people from controlling how you follow and obey the God who sent you in the first place. Any system, organization, person, place, or thing that's unwilling to honor you is disqualified for any relationship.

As a leader, I find it ironic that other leaders criticize people who self-promote. If they are refused honor and support in the relationships and systems they serve, who else will promote them? When God has promoted you and your leader can't even hear the promotion, that's a problem. Honestly, the same people telling you not to self-promote have every social media tool and gadget to promote themselves. That is manipulation and control. They're doing the thing they are telling you not to. Countless times I've seen ungodly systems set up where faithful people have to go through a man-made process to be recognized and supported. You can't tell me that I have to go through 19 classes to be recognized, after being committed to the church for 19 years. I know, first hand, the frustration that accompanies this level of dishonor.

I never asked anybody to ordain me as an apostle or prophet. I never sought out a man to ordain me. God opened my understanding of the life of Jesus and David, so I did the work. I traveled to many nations. After doing the work I realized I was an apostolic voice in the nations. I had developed sons and daughters. A man I wasn't in covenant with saw me and approached me to affirm me an apostle of divine arts for the work I'd already done. He didn't know me from a can of paint.

45

Sadly, the people I had been with for years wouldn't even affirm me as a janitor. What was I waiting for? I'm in my early 50s and would have still been waiting if I had continued to sit there. There was no reason for me not to be endorsed or affirmed. Often times, leaders will unfairly gauge their endorsement of you by comparing you to others. What does someone else's life have to do with God's system? Are we to follow man's system or obedience to God? Man will always fail when it comes to those two in my life. Now, you may be tempted to snarl at that statement, but my obedience to God trumps any and everything. Even after doing all the proper things to get released, I still was not released. I said it already; there is no right way to leave in a Saul system. You can write a 10-page essay explaining how God has given you to leave. It doesn't matter. If they so desire, they will *still* bad mouth you. In fact, your pastor should never determine when it's time for you to leave and obey God. You should and would know that before them anyway. Leaders that serve more than 10 members don't have a schedule that permits them to keep up with everything in their own lives and destinies, let alone yours. We can't fake like we have it all together. It's impossible to juggle and manage everything that comes up with being a leader. Wise leaders will honestly admit they don't have the capacity to govern whether it's time for you to obey God. There is liberty in honesty and transparency. It's impossible to govern 100 spiritual sons and daughters.

Leaders don't even have time to interact with every member on Sunday morning. They have to get an appointment just to interact with you. So, why do we perpetrate like God has shown us the blueprint for every member? God doesn't even operate in that manner. For those who allow this to happen to them, let me admonish you not to be so star struck that you make excuses for controlling behavior. We make excuses for leaders and don't keep them accountable. The Saul system causes you to make excuses for some and release condemnation over others. For instance, if I as a leader, don't call you back after I've promised to, one would say I don't have integrity. If that happens from someone you're impressed by, you make the excuse that they are busy. That's the picture of a Saul system.

Saul's system doesn't want to endorse anyone it can't control. That sounds astounding, but it's such a proven fact. Increasingly, leaders become wounded when people make a decision to leave. They are also in denial that they refused to release people, based on selfish reasons. Their feelings tend to justify their actions, stating that they feel betrayed, but that's a contradiction. How are you feeling betrayed when you should've released them in the first place? Who suffered the most; the person that sought to obey God or the leader who is hurt? The story becomes, "I poured into them...I had them in my house," etc. Then the church is left choosing sides. The unfortunate thing is, when we lead by our emotions, we don't realize the damage we do to people's reputation. We act like someone is such a bad person because they chose to obey God. We do not have the right to discredit people out of a place of offense. It's evil for you to not tell the truth about a member's decision to leave, as it causes people to paint their own picture. Your silence produces a lie, and that is evil. What you produce is people treating them indifferent and you allow people to make inferences about their character.

I've witnessed how the Saul system will sabotage you to leaders that you have a mutual relationship with. If they are led by their emotions, all they have to do is get on the phone and call people to say, "Don't bring them in." This is why your dependence should not solely be on other people to open doors for you because they can close them just as quickly as they opened them. The Saul system couldn't control my contacts because they weren't adjacent to my leaders. I'd established relationships with churches on my own, but those doors adjacent to leaders who discredited me were closed. We'll sit up and talk about how treacherous the world is, but the same system is at work in the church.

I had to learn some of these lessons the hard way. We have people who are blockers. When they see your ministry building momentum, they will get on the phone and block it. Anyone who has a false reproach on their name or stands on the side of truth mirrors Christ.

Jesus stood in the flow of the temple's money. Standing on the side of truth affects the flow of money, and you will be shut down for it. Jezebel came on the scene to block Israel's momentum. She destroyed prophetic worship and discredited who people were (I Kings 18). I've seen leaders invite someone to teach in their church on the down low, but will block them from preaching in their pulpit. Everywhere I went, I was treated with skepticism by leaders. No effort was made to get to know me. It took some of the young people to tell me things that were said about me. A teenager came to me and said, "I just don't see what we've been warned about you." This is why when you are Davidic, you don't have to prove anything about yourself. God can't protect you when you choose to retaliate or defend yourself. To the religious folks who don't seek God but depend on the pastor to tell them everything, realize that a prophet hath no honor in his own home.

Restoring Identity to Judah

When people finally discover who they are, they can no longer be misused and controlled. Judah is often hurt because of the improper use of them as a gift. Leaders, you are hurting Judah by having the gift serve you more than serving God. When Judah refuses to be misused any longer and leaves, the mourning of the leader comes from the fact that they can't use Judah anymore. They will try anything to keep you from leaving, including manipulating you with promises of promotion. A boss keeps you on a job with a promise of future promotion. A father and son dynamic do not do that. A father helps prepare you by releasing and affirming you- not manipulating you and keeping you stagnant because of jealousy. Their sadness comes from the denial of improper use. Everyone isn't your son. I found that many relationships I had with older men of God thought they were in ministry longer than me and that made them a father. They underestimated me and thought I was just a musician. But I traveled in ministry with my father as a child. They wanted me to submit to them as a son, but they didn't have what I needed as a father. Then I found many of them weren't fathered. They started their ministry out of rebellion. They expected me to do things they couldn't themselves.

We try to manipulate people using the word with Scriptures that don't apply to the situation. If we use appropriate Scripture in the Saul and David dynamic, we would see your fingertips on the javelin- not mine. Yet, they use Scripture to manipulate like that. You use it incorrectly, thinking you're exempt, because of your status and title. That's wrong. Saul wants people to agree with him, not challenge him. No one is allowed to disagree or challenge. No one is allowed to have a brain. God doesn't get glory out of making clones that can't think on their own. Remember the portrait of a godly father in David. He identified his sons and

but also?

50

daughters and allowed their fathers to identify them, so they could operate in their gift with accuracy. On the contrary, people operating in a Saul system won't identify you, because they don't want you to know who you are. Knowing who you truly are stops them from having control over you.

Corruption in the Camp

In the Saul system, it looks like the only person preaching is the set man. The Saul system has a house prophet. The Saul system has a favorite singer, instead of an anointed minstrel. That singer or person compromises and does all the leader wants even when it's wrong (and you know it's wrong). You know you're in compromise and the only reason you don't speak up is they are padding your pocket to keep quiet. Prophets are getting paid to prophesy and intercessors are getting paid to pray. That's often a tool to keep you from revealing what's hidden in your camp. Prophets nowadays cannot correct the church in its ordinances. The Saul system makes you a soothsayer, not a prophet. All you are releasing is soothing words. You cry that your church is the best, but you're the worst one because you refuse to deal with the issues. You dance and praise over your iniquities. If you dare challenge the foolishness in the church today, you are automatically marked for death. The first thing they will kill is your influence, and the second is your ability to think on your own. When you go to a leader and say, "I think God is telling me…" you're going to get a fight. Your strongest resistance is from those you think you're in covenant with. That's a result of them thinking they have a preconceived notion about you anyway. So, what you say is compromised. You can feel the negative representation of misunderstanding. Everybody doesn't have or understand the standard of truth. Even as I say this, I can hear someone say, "You're not Jesus and it's impossible to live like Jesus." That's a lie for people making excuses not to live like Jesus. The way of a transgressor is hard. It's really not that hard. Be real! David gives us the example that we should be creatures who the enemy can never tell on. We should be telling on ourselves. We should admit the truth of ourselves. I tell God what I honestly feel and my struggles. Then I tell Him to help me with that area.

[handwritten margin note: I would say that well except through the Spirit.]

The purpose of this book exposing all these facets of praise and worship is that Judah must go first to win this battle. If you haven't noticed, we are losing right now. There is a great misuse of our authority and influence. Yet, we want people to follow us as we follow God. We need to start here in Judah and repent so we can move forward and be triumphant. So, leaders let us restore the honor and identity of those God honors. Let us eliminate the corrupt mishandling of one another in the Body. Let the minstrels play and let the anointed psalmists sing so they can be who they are and you can be who you are.

Chapter Three
The Vehicle to Reform

The tabernacle of David is a picture of how God wants us to live our life in 24-hour worship. The picture is simple. God wants us to obey Him, as worship is obedience. Worship is not the musical selection(s) we offer in our worship services. Worship is the offering of our lives, 24 hours a day- not only when it's convenient. It is a vehicle 24 hours a day- not when you need it or when you come to church.

To resurrect the tabernacle of David, every moment of our lives, is to show how we can access wealth and health. David gave to everybody that was in need. He provided something for everybody. We don't think along those lines. We build our individual kingdoms, but claim we represent the King.

Prophetic Worship

The purpose of prophetic worship is to display that we serve a God who talks back to us. The rejection of prophetic worship is based on an excuse to support disobedience to the Word of the Lord. Leaders will say, "Give the people what they want and sing songs everyone knows." Yet, worship isn't for the people. God wants to speak to us through prophetic worship, as it releases where the flow of the Spirit is now. Prophetic worship sings of His heart, His love, His purpose, and His will. On the other hand, learned songs often connect you with the experience of the author. That's why most learned songs are inspired by a certain situation and not by a relationship with God. David sang often about his relationship with Father. Those songs were inspired by relationship. That's why God addressed Him as "a man after God's own heart" (I Samuel 13:14, Acts 13:22). God is a spontaneous God. Everything about Him is prophetic. You sing to Him and He sings back to you through the song of the Lord. I'm sure some of the readers were looking for a theological, Bible teacher's approach on this topic, but I don't talk in those terms. I preach and teach based on my relationship with God. All the Bible verses you can come up with Are WELL-KNOWN and I don't write to prove all the Scriptures I know. I leave you the responsibility to search out the matter for yourself in the Word. We have become so used to people doing everything for us. Yet, God tore the veil so we could have access for ourselves. The veil is torn so that you can have access to God and hear from Him.

Our church is made of needy people waiting for the pastors okay to do anything. We can't pick out a brand of corn flakes without asking the pastor. You call your pastors and ask when it's okay for you to visit your family. That's foolishness. I'm hammering this area because we need reform. God is trying to show us that the things we did in the past are not only absurd, but are not working. We seek direction from our pastors more than we seek it from God. It's the difference in AM and FM. AM frequency (most churches are on) is asking mode. We can't hear Him in this mode because we only approach Him to ask for something. The antenna is so weak the signal is distorted. We keep asking because we don't believe. God is trying to shift us to FM (fulfillment mode), where the sound is clear. The antenna is larger through relationship. In this mode your relationship with God is the conduit that fulfills you. When you ask for something or seek for direction, you already know it's done. This is how we get to a place of reform- by allowing God to shift us to fulfillment mode through intimate relationship with Him.

Prophetic worship is a way of God speaking through His people. We are the only Kingdom that has a God that can speak back. Who would serve a God that you can't hear? As I stated earlier, music, frequencies, and sound enter without permission. When it's played into your life, it enters faster. Answers you've been waiting on in your life can get to you through prophetic worship. God's not interested in wasting time (although He is time and made time). He's not interested in wasting oil either. What we see being done by the majority is not as healthy as the minority. Just because I see an exhaustive percentage of America smoking weed, doesn't mean that I need to start. Majority means nothing to me. Doing something because everybody else is doing it isn't a good reason to do anything.

I want you all to understand a new song provokes a new nature, while an old song keeps an old nature around. Let me prove my point. When you hear a song that's old, there is usually a memory attached to it. When you sing a new song, you just created a memory. Somebody look at your neighbor and say, "Reform!"

Essentially, what I'm trying to convey to everyone who reads this book is that authenticity is so important. When you remain authentic and appreciate who and what God made you, you will always produce things that are original. You will not have to waste your time perpetrating yourself as someone you admire. The only time people do that is when they are not happy with who they are. When my angels have to deliver a package to me, I don't want them to be confused, because I'm trying to be somebody else. Selah. It's easy to be yourself. It's difficult trying to mimic others. This is also the result of someone being mentored. You're usually being cloned by the person mentoring you. When you disciple someone, you teach them to be like Christ. Christ said these are my disciples- not mentees. You shape and mold what a person becomes by what you speak into their lives. There is also power in what you say. This is why when churches speak that they will always have the best singers and musicians, that's all they get. They need to say, "I want the best minstrels and psalmists because their hearts are after God."

The church has to transition over to the mind of God, not the pattern we've seen before by uninformed men acting out of learned behavior. I am talking about the biblical blueprint that only comes from time in the Word and in the presence of God. No man or woman will ever know how God wants it if we don't ask. We perpetuate the way everyone else did it: momma, daddy, grandmamma, and Reverend so and so. However, that's tradition, and those traditions didn't even work for them. If we are truly honest, we'd admit that they died defeated and unfulfilled. Because of sentimental reason, we refuse to accept that *The Old Ship of Zion* didn't work for them. Very few of us want to admit that. My mother was prophetic and was more accurate than many men that worked to shut her down because women were only seen as capable of serving them chicken. Why would God wait on some of us men to get in place to further His agenda? He won't. He will use whoever makes themselves available. I'm tired of men hating instead of relating. Get in obedience and get in your place. There is enough work to go around. There are enough souls to go around. There are enough platforms to go around. There is enough of everything to go around and for you to fulfill your assignment.

I believe musicians and psalmists should be in the Kingdom, not just the church. That's two different functions. They were created to serve the Kingdom and Kingdom agenda, not just a local church. The Kingdom is vast, but the church is secluded. The church is founded and run on the preference of the leader. The Kingdom is wherever you set your foot. The church was meant to be in this state, but nobody ever wants to leave the building.

Music Myths

Let me kill the myth about what music is of the devil and of God. All styles of music were created by man, but every ability to create the styles was given by God. So, there is no certain style that trumps all sound. If that's the truth, there would be no need for God to shoulder the need for diversity. The diversity we see in Earth is the diversity in Heaven. There is no Black, White, or Hispanic music. I believe different genres of music were created to reach different people. So, if you are apostolic, you should be able to reach all people groups. I use to travel throughout a lot of emerging countries. When interpreters fell under the Holy Spirit, they left me hanging. When I worshiped, I leaned into the sound the Lord was releasing in that region. I refused to force our westernized culture down their throats. We're giving them not what they know, but what they need. In the islands, the worship that comes out of me is reggae, raga, or Caribbean. It's not forced; it's what Holy Spirit leads me to. If I'm in the area where country music is being played, I usually am led to play a sound that is country music. That's RAW: Real Apostolic Worship.

Ignorant Statements Made

I need to address some of the ignorant statements that are made concerning all things worship. The list consists of the following:
- "The praise team wasn't in there."
- "They weren't flowing today."
- "They didn't take me in."
- "I don't know what was wrong with them; they were dry."

These are the most popular asinine statements about worship from people who don't know who and what worship is for. Praise and worship is not for *you* in the first place. If you would spend more time in the presence of God, before you get to church, no one lol not where I thought he was going.

mmm

would have to tell you that. You wouldn't even have to
be corrected by this book- telling you the ignorance in
making a statement about people who are serving you.
They are not even meant to serve you, but to serve God.
Yet, our lack of understanding has erected a system
that has to become seeker-friendly, to make you happy.
Praise and worship was never meant to make your
natural ears satisfied. Your ears are trained to hear
what sounds good. If you've ever spoken one of the
above statements, it shows how low your love level is.
Whether they sound good or not, why can't you discern
their heart in trying to offer God their best? If your
heart was pure, you would engage, instead of gauging
their ability. These statements come from people who
are critical and come to a worship setting to critique.
Your worship team would never measure up because
they aren't doing it for you. This is so freeing for Judah
because man's findings are not important in the
interaction where praise and worship were meant for
the King.

Putting the Responsibility Back Where It Belongs

It was never the responsibility of the worship
leader(s) to touch the hearts of the people. It was also
never their responsibility to "take you in" or help you
get your breakthrough. This responsibility is and has
always belonged to Holy Spirit. Worship leaders, you
are responsible to be the first to go in, before others.

They shouldn't merely be told to do what they see you do. They should see you do it. They should see you go in first. Yet, the responsibility does not fall on you alone. As the worship leader goes in, the congregation (leaders and laypersons alike) should worship together as a unified corporate body.

In the mention of spiritual gifts, apostles are listed first. Therefore, apostles, you should be the first to do what's expected in everything, especially in worship. The apostle is supposed to do, first, what every other five-fold ministry gift is expected to do. Jesus said, "I only do what I see my Father do." So if I see my Father worshiping, then I should do it. My Father shouldn't have to tell me what to do. Animals have more sense to do what they see their leaders do. How is it that animals have no problem doing what they were created to do, but we refuse to? When we treat worship as the last on the priority list, we can expect the worship to be a lacking priority. We have conferences about everything but worship. We should be conferenced out and tired of the money-exchange game.

Things that are important (like prayer and praise and worship), no one shows up to, because it's not important to them. Leaders, your congregation isn't going to be interested in anything that you're disinterested in. How do you expect your congregation to be worshipers when they don't see you worship? You don't even come out during worship.

Because of the wrong foundation we've set, we've given the responsibility of the band and singers to lead people into a place where they've never been before. If your relationship with God, love for Jesus, and dependence on the Holy Ghost doesn't lead you to worship, then we (minstrels and singers) are just manipulating you and what you're offering up to God is just fake. To be honest, the greatest worship service should be at your house and in your intimate time with God. However, the reality is that most of us do not think about worship until Sunday service. We are to live a life of worship. We are supposed to be glory-carriers. Instead of arriving at church expecting the team to manufacture the glory, what part of the glory did you bring? If you're a true worshiper, bring something to the table. Don't come looking to "get" all the time. If you don't have anything to bring, offer yourself. That's what He wants anyway. We're good at saying and singing catchy songs like, *I Give Myself Away*, but we can't even give stuff away in our closet to those in need.

Judah free yourself. It is not the praise and worship leaders or minstrel's responsibility that people get what they need in worship. It's wrong for leaders to put this type of burden on people. It was never meant for man, but for God. It is not their responsibility to bring in your wandering minds. That's religion. Most of the things we do in church is a result of learned behavior, and not seeking the face of God. We pattern things after the majority, not the minority, which is a reflection of the Saul system, not the Davidic order.

Psalmists, free yourselves. Embrace the song of the Lord and release prophetic songs from Heaven. When your heart is pure and you don't know any better, you're free, because what you release came from God. God told me, "Leave the results up to me, Jacques. You just be obedient." We're so worried about people responding to us. That's not our responsibility. If you don't hear your favorite song when I worship, it wasn't for you anyway and I'm happy to disappoint you. You can never be mad that you're disappointing man when you choose to please God. If you're pleasing man, you're displeasing God.

Minstrels, free yourselves. Stop worrying about if what you're playing or if the timing of what you're playing is correct. All God requires is that you make yourself available. He'll do the rest. He'll flow through you. If too much of you is present, He can't get through you. This is why, even with my prophetic band, I don't allow us to rehearse. Your rehearsal should be your lifestyle. Your rehearsal should be working on your relationship, not your chops. The problem in all areas of ministry has been wrong teaching. We've been taught to sharpen our gifts and not our character. The gift-giver is perfect, so anything He gives is perfect. It doesn't need any perfecting. Your character is what needs to be sharpened and perfected. This is what we are to work on when we are off the stage. This is why

Scripture clearly states, "Gifts and callings come without repentance" (Romans 11:29). It's not because the gift needs to repent, it's because it came from God and was already perfected. The sharpening of your gift only breeds competition between you and the next person. Touch your neighbor and say, "Reform!"

In all things, when God is requiring you to keep your authenticity, it is because He is requiring you to be a trendsetter and not a trend follower. Most trends today are not of God. No person is alike. Even identical twins have something different about them. That tells me God never intended for us to pattern ourselves or our ways after another. The only thing He required is for us to pattern our ways after His son-which was himself made flesh.

Chapter Four
The Role of Minstrels

The original biblical intention and purpose of the minstrel was to entertain the King. Even after creation, they were used in the carnal arena to entertain kings. While doing so, all kings could be refreshed. There are several accounts where God created situations to use the minstrel. You'll find it was because of the minstrels that prophets were activated. They are used to trouble the prophetic waters and stir things up. Prophets benefited from their encounter with minstrels. It put them on a completely different level. Minstrels stir up the prophetic waters. Psalmists and prophets, then, interpret what has been stirred.

Minstrels were never meant to be controlled by a leader or expeditor. They are not one's personal musical accompaniment. They are meant to follow Holy Spirit's leading. If you can't lead them and guide them musically, how do you control them? If you cannot articulate something taking place in the spirit, be quiet. Most times, leaders want to bring a sound they're familiar with from their private time into the corporate arena of worship. This is out of order. A real minstrel is usually an individual who God has anointed to master the arts of following and leading at the same time. Because their endowment came from Holy Spirit and their relationship is with Jesus, they cannot be controlled. They will follow God at any cost and leave you standing looking silly. A musician is only motivated by what's in the envelope handed to them after he or she plays. A minstrel is motivated by the promises of God, whether you hand them an envelope or not. They can function either way- knowing that God is their source. They are creatures that refuse to compromise.

Psalmists are never supposed to lead a minstrel or dictate where the minstrel is supposed to go because they've never been there. The minstrel received the direction concerning where to go and prophesies it with their hands. There is a passage that describes Elisha inquiring of a minstrel to help him hear direction from the Lord on the behalf of Israel. "But now bring me a minstrel. And it came to pass, when the minstrel played, that the hand of the Lord came upon him. And he (Elisha) said, Thus saith the Lord (2 Kings 3:15-16)." They sent for the minstrel, and as he was playing, direction was sent from the Lord. The minstrel is used to trouble the water. The psalmist is supposed to just jump in it, not navigate it. Not even leaders are supposed to do this. If minstrels could be navigated, there would've been no reason to send forth Judah first. Even in a corporate setting, when a minstrel and psalmist are together, there is no confusion. There is harmony when each allows the other to function in the capacity they were graced for. That's why psalmists are sometimes out there by themselves because they ran off and left the minstrel. This is out of order. If minstrels are meant to follow the psalmist, there's no need for the minstrel to be there. Here is an example of what that looks like. In the 90s I used to run into prophets and prophetesses who would embarrass me by saying, "Change the flow" and "Give me warfare music." I'm thinking, what is warfare music? Then when you play something, they would say that is not it. They would disrupt the flow God gave us (minstrels) to play the flow they wanted. They created confusion by disrupting what God was doing, to demand their preference. After the disruption, the Lord brought us right back where we were before we were disrupted by the "famous gift." In another incident, the same person did it again after having a discussion with them about the disrespect of shutting someone down and making them less confident about hearing the Lord. When they did it again, I packed up my keyboard and I left. They wanted me to change the music, so I changed it. Minstrels, know that you are not dogs and are not there to accommodate "the gift." There should be mutual respect for the people that serve. You don't get to disrespect people because you have a title or a name. No man or woman is obligated to be dishonored. Now, that's what I did. I'm not suggesting that, but it's what I did. I'm not going to stand for it. I am a minister just like you are. When you don't understand the purpose of people in their perspective graces, you will always abuse them. If people understood that according to the biblical usage, God loved minstrels so much that He created situations to use them. They play for God. They are for His usage, not yours. They are not your personal musician or employee, or to cater to you. That's abuse. Again, when you don't know the purpose of a thing, you'll abuse it. It's not the fault of the psalmists when they've been trained through the eyes of people who preach learned behavior and not truth. They've only followed the training of the preacher in his set plan, not God's.

Psalmists that don't know any better are not to blame. Leaders who know better need to teach better. Teaching like this disrupts their kingdoms and plans and takes the focus off of them- putting it back on God. They don't want their structures demolished. This is why a lot of leaders fight prophetic worship. It eliminates the excuse of, "We should be singing something everybody knows." In all actuality, everybody knows God, so we should be singing what God wants. What about Him? He is the priority in worship. Pastors have said, "I don't want these types of songs, because people don't participate." Just because we sing songs everyone knows, it doesn't mean that you're on one accord.

When the presence of God comes in through worship, it should expose who you really are. A pump or prime should not be needed to worship the God you say you love. God wants to know how long will we sing over our iniquities? How long will we manufacture a presence that has nothing to do with God? It's only emotion and dancing over our emotions. Why should I have to motivate you to worship a God that wakes you up each morning? You praise and worship Him not out of obligation, but because you love Him. You don't do it because your pastor told you to.

Diversity of Minstrels

I want to share with you the other uses of minstrels in this hour. Minstrels should be trained to do housecleaning. Holy Spirit trained me to take my keyboard, set it up, and worship in a home a person was to purchase, to clean out evil spirits that took residence in the home. Minstrels should also do this in the church. Holy Spirit had me go two hours before a service and play in the building where I was to minister. He told me if He could trust me to play before Him, He could trust me not to perform before man. The benefit of doing this is, whatever ungodly spirits were there, you'll get them out before service. You are a minstrel for the King and you get the atmosphere ready to prepare for the King. The problem is, we don't prepare for the King to come. We prepare for the guest speaker to come.

Minstrel Armor Bearer

It is a minstrel/armor bearer that gives the expediter the right weapons to fight with at the right moment. As the minstrel plays he or she connects the activity in Heaven with the Earth realm. That comes from a consecrated lifestyle. Minstrels have to prepare like a preacher prepares to preach a sermon. Whatever is taking place in the Spirit is played through the instrument and speakers to the people. All the people that David came in contact with benefited from his lifestyle.

Minstrel Scribe

This minstrel is one who can take the songs of the Lord and refine, arrange, and turn them into songs of corporate worship. This minstrel may also be able to take the arrangement and turn it into a learned song. It takes a grace to accomplish this.

Apostolic Minstrel

There is a diversity of minstrels that are apostolic in nature. Though they are usually apostolic, they are not recognized by people who want to keep them a musician. That form of dishonor stems from jealousy. These minstrels are multitalented individuals. They usually have the spiritual DNA of David and Jesus. Both of them functioned in all five-fold gifts but didn't have to be called either one of them. These minstrels can do anything they are called to do. Apostolic minstrels activate people, send people, pastor people, and thrust people. This type of minstrel is one of the most evangelical because their heart is for souls. This is a picture of who God has made me. I didn't choose to be any of these. I was chosen. I would rather be in the streets evangelizing, instead of in the four walls of the church.

These are the minstrels God is raising up to change the whole climate for the Kingdom, as we know it. They will be used more so in the house churches than in the church house. Our church houses are glamorous. They don't want effective people. These minstrels are also usually attacked by the Saul spirit and system because what they carry is an anointing that aggravates the evil spirits in the Saul's. When you come in contact with someone with David's DNA you can't help but be aggravated. A lot of minstrels and musicians won't agree with this. It's okay; you can disagree with truth, but it's still the truth. Let God be true and every man a liar. It's the Word.

The minstrels and psalmists who function like I described above should always have a strong intercessory and accountability base. You are a direct target of the enemy. We don't have people to teach this. Why wouldn't you be a target when you're able to do what the enemy couldn't do and be faithful doing it? He hates you. That's why you can't have mixture in your life. God doesn't do anything illegal and doesn't allow the enemy to do anything illegal. That's why the enemy makes suggestions, not commands. You are in control, but if he suggests and you do it, you give the enemy access. Remember saints, things are never difficult unless you are still trying instead of doing.

The Mystery of the Minstrel

Minstrels are not welcome in an atmosphere that it is controlled by a Jezebel system. The system cannot operate in an atmosphere where there is a pure flow. That's why people always say, "Change the flow," as they need their own spiritual climate to function. They come in and treat the flow a minstrel releases as "You missed it," or "I'm going to show you something." They need to sit down. They do this to take the attention off of them, as it uncovers that they are not where they should be. We see this in a competitive atmosphere where leaders and/or preachers become jealous of minstrels and psalmists because they can't do what minstrels and psalmists can do. However, minstrels and psalmists can do everything leaders and preachers do. This is the Davidic and Saulic dynamic. Saul was jealous of David because he could play, sing, and win victories. David changed the whole nation with his worship, not his itinerary. David accomplished more through his obedience than Saul did. What made Saul upset with him is he knew dirt on David, yet he was still favored. This is why your pastor can't understand why you are so effective, even after the things you shared with them in private.

The minstrel was something dear to God's heart. So much so that He created situations to use them. The evil spirit in Saul, God put it in Him so He could use David to play it out of him. The characteristics of a minstrel were that they were cunning, skillful, and full of the Spirit of God. Their access to portals in the Spirit comes from their obedience, not their talent. Skill has nothing to do with how many notes they can play at one time. It is their ability to yield and listen to Holy Spirit at the same time. It's not about their chords or chops, but how they live from day to day.

Minstrels are generally more likely to be covenant people with the organization or ministry they play for. They are not bouncing from place to place to get a paycheck. Because of the lack of honor in the body of Christ for Judah, minstrels usually have to play more than one place. This is because most leaders don't believe in paying on their minstrel's heart-level but on their talent. So, minstrels are forced to maintain other means of making money (like playing in other churches). This tends to cause a distraction in their commitment to spend time with God. David didn't put minstrels on salary, he bought the land so that they didn't have distractions and could spend time with God. I've heard leaders tell minstrels to go get a job when the topic of needing a raise comes up. However, the demand asks the minstrel to spend 70% of his time at the church, but they are only compensated for 30% of their time. Out of ignorance, we should not ask people to do something we're not willing to do ourselves.

A minstrel usually cannot articulate to you how God uses them. Every time a minstrel sits down to a keyboard, they don't know where God is taking them or where they are going. Now, that's if God is truly using them. So, if Holy Spirit doesn't tell the minstrel where they are going, how can a leader or someone expediting a service tell them where to go? A minstrel needs to be free to follow Holy Spirit. They need not be manipulated by someone who is trying to steer them. Minstrels (male or female) yield their vessels and God uses them. They don't know how to do anything else.

It's been my experience that other ministry gifts think they know more about a minstrel's gift than they do. I've seen intercessors try to tell minstrels what to play when they are praying. It's also been my experience that intercessors enter the worship service after minstrels, who are at sound check playing before the Lord long before intercessors arrive. Then they show up asking for warfare music. Honestly, the warfare is in your head, because you're late. I still haven't been able to figure out what warfare music is, anyway. There are times when the minstrel is playing and the intercessor tells them to stop playing. Then they tell the minstrel later to start playing again or that they are not playing what they want. Whether intentional or unintentional, this behavior toys with and manipulates the minstrel's ability to hear. Frankly, the minstrels become shut down.

I've seen celebrity preachers come in who had a bad day or bad flight and take it out on the minstrels. Then they say, "What you were playing was not conducive to what I wanted to do." Guest preacher, you told on yourself. You wanted to do what you wanted to do- not what Holy Spirit wants to do. The expeditor does not manipulate the minstrels. The minstrels are to stir the waves in the water, and the people enter.

I strongly believe God created the minstrel to preserve the Body of Christ, as well as their natural bodies. Here is the illustration: As David played to the soil and produced, he also played to the dirt that we were formed out of. I believe the minstrel is created to preserve our body. The reason our deliverance ministries are not as effective as they could be is that the young people playing have been listening to music in the secular arena that is demonic. We need Spirit-filled minstrels who can play it out of them. I've seen high-tech devils. You have to have a relationship with the King to get this stuff out. Babies are sneaking to listen to today's demonic music. If it wasn't demonic, why would they need to sneak to listen to these artists?

One of the signature characteristics of minstrels is suffering. They are professional sufferers, and if they yield to the King, they will become professional overcomers. The distinctive attribute in a minstrel's life is the understanding that they have to prepare. A minstrel understands nothing is done by accident. They understand their purpose and do things on purpose. When minstrels possess a prayer life, they should never know a life of poverty, unless they are being dishonored. It's impossible. It's impossible for there to be poverty around minstrels that open up the Heavens and cause their sphere of influence to experience an open Heaven. They create open Heavens and should experience an open Heaven in every area of their lives.

Frequencies

Music is the only thing that you don't need permission or a permit to go into the soil. It is a frequency. Think about it; we've been force fed sound in our radios or environments, whether we like it or not. It comes through the speaker. This is why, as an apostle of divine arts, when I come into a church, I can hear details of what's going on in the church through the sound in the speakers. When leaders are complaining about a lot of things, the source is usually the music. This is where it usually starts. There is no way you can sit under pure worship and not be affected by it. You can't even sit under what's foul and not be affected by it. Frequencies are all around us. Whatever frequency you have around you, you respond to it. Sin is a frequency. It affects how you spend your money. Music is used in the grocery store to make you buy what you shouldn't be buying.

The purpose of God anointing minstrels is to help the church get on (and stay on) the right frequency to hear Him. Minstrels set the church on the frequency to hear Him and differentiate from the voice of humanity. God used the minstrels to provoke hearing and speaking through His prophets, not to preach a message. Instead of allowing this to happen in our churches, we shut it down because leaders and programs can't control it.

I am a firm believer that if we are proclaiming to be the Kingdom and not just the church, we should operate on a royal structure. By that I mean, minstrels and psalmists should be imparted and hands laid on them to identify their function in the Kingdom. They should be identified and effectively reared. This will eliminate the hireling spirit and eliminate getting a person in your music ministry whose only commitment is to the dollar.

Judah is built according to a royal structure. Royals do not decide what they'll be, it's decided for them. Whether you are a prophet, psalmist, and/or minstrel, your fathers (natural and spiritual) should invest in you as a child and bless you in that function as well. They should bestow honor on them in their callings of royalty. It's a proven fact that anyone who lives with being dishonored for a period of time can be opened up to disease. I've experienced this in my own life. As a minstrel, I was dishonored. Getting a closer relationship with God caused me to look to Him for accolades because I wasn't getting them from others. My innocence is what saved my life. I didn't know any better and wasn't smart enough to know I was being dishonored; I just wanted God. That's why one of the attributes of a minstrel is that they are not people of learned behavior. They never pick up on others' behavior or pattern themselves after it. They stand out as being weird. The sounds they produce are authentic. David was and maintained his authenticity. He made sure those around him kept their authenticity, as well.

There should be some type of respect for a chief musician that is set in a place or region. When I go into a jurisdiction, I ask the chief musician if it's okay if I minister. It is wise to place honor on them so that there are no hindrances and you can play freely. I honor the person over the music by asking if it's okay for me to minister in the area that they've been given jurisdiction. It kills backlash and retaliation because you're honoring the set gift. Enact the honor system. Equally, when you're brought into a place, you honor a region.

The Sound God is Requiring

I'm sure a lot of you hear a lot of ministry gifts say they hear a particular sound. That's a myth. If there was a particular sound produced because of your ethnicity, then why is there diversity in Heaven? A lot of us will get to Heaven and be disappointed to find out that the music in Heaven does not cater to our ethnicity. The sound God is requiring is the condition of your heart. That's what creates the sound God is looking for. Man is looking for a sound that is more like his preference. God requires us to sing to Him a new song. It's a sound neither of us has ever heard, but He heard it because He created it. Our inclination is to gravitate toward our preference. When we assemble together, we are supposed to sing what God wants to hear. Scripture says, "Sing unto the Lord a new song" (Psalm 96:1). We are so stubborn; we make excuses to do what we want. We blame the congregation and say they want songs that are familiar to them. If they say that (which I don't believe they do), they need to be taught correctly as much as we need to govern ourselves to adhere to what God wants. He wants to be sung new songs. We have more confidence in the world and what the Gospel arena is doing than what God is doing. We treat God and the Bible like a menu. We take only what we want.

Minstrels Tap into Realms

I often ran into a lot of ministry gifts who had little or no understanding of the realms that minstrels tap into. They don't understand and we honestly don't understand it, until we live it out. There are countless encounters of supernatural revivals that have taken place in America where greedy men of God have capitalized off praise and worship teams and minstrels who have tapped into portals. The leaders were greedy, in that they took credit for the portals opened by psalmists and minstrels, and kept the revivals going to collect the money. They never gave credit to the access psalmists and minstrels possess to produce these portals and, in turn, release revival.

When David played for Saul to be relieved from the evil spirit, God moved through David's hands on his instrument. The minstrel causes the hand of God to move. In David's encounter with Saul, God laid His hands directly on Saul. This is what the minstrel does, he or she moves the hand of God. In my experience, every time that something of that magnitude was about to happen, some leader shut it down, because they didn't understand it. I've been accused of shifting the service because the leader has no control. No one should have control in the Lord's service. We lie and tell God, "God have your way." Then when He does, we blame it on the minstrel. God was having His way, but you shut it down. The beauty of being on the right frequency and functioning biblically is you get right results. This is why we need more people to teach and activate people on these things. Everyone needs to be taught- not segregated. Often we have private sessions taught on sound, accessing realms, prophetic dance, or flags. However, the congregation doesn't know what is being taught and has never heard these principles. They need to be taught along with Judah. Judah is treated like a Sunday School message, as it's kept from being preached from the pulpit, but confined to a private classroom. It is not prioritized.

As a church it saddens me that we do not value the ministry gift of minstrels. Musicians are skilled to play what you tell them to play, but minstrels have the ability to take it far beyond that. I can prove this point in the secular arena, alone. Prince, Michael Jackson, R. Kelly, and Beyoncé excelled in ways that many other skillful musicians haven't. In fact, they were supposed to be worship leaders. They have/had automatic charisma from birth. Most people that are sold out to God are attacked and marked by poverty. Yet, in the secular arena, those that are sold out are given riches. The enemy wants those that are sold out to God to compromise. The deception is this; he wants you to come to the world to get something your Father already owns. That's backward. I don't need anything if I have to get it that way. I say all the time, "How can the devil offer me something that my Father already owns?" Singers and musicians always fall for that. Satan dangles those things in your face. Too often we struggle to wait for God to give it to us because it takes longer than we want to wait. God knows your future and what's ahead, and He knows your unwillingness to surrender. In my early days, there were things I was not privy to because I was not willing to surrender to God. I wasn't giving Him glory. I was too happy to take credit for things that belonged to Him. I wanted to hear *my* name praised. I wanted to hear people cheer me on. So He restricted me from realms and access because He knew it would kill me. I would've literally lost my life. This taught me you can be used by God and not be a son. For all theologians who want proof of that statement; God uses the devil. Enough said. As a minstrel, I decided that it's not enough for me to be used by God. I want to be a son.

Minstrel vs. Hireling

A hireling spirit never wants to be in covenant with anyone, because it wants to be free to play where the highest bidder appears. They are never faithful because someone could come and offer more money and they would be gone. They usually don't even give a notice. They are not faithful. On the contrary, a minstrel will stay where they feel they can build. They usually are led by Holy Spirit in everything they do. The conflict comes in because they are not novices to spiritual things. David, as a minstrel, benefited different leaders because of his relationship with God. Nowadays, most leaders don't think that they can benefit from someone who doesn't have a church or someone they don't see as their equal. At times, what provoked jealousy in my life was that I could do everything my pastor could do, but they couldn't do what I was gifted to do. Instead of embracing that I was there to help, they allowed their jealousy to attempt to suppress me. This was the David and Saul dynamic at work again. Most people operating out of a Saul dynamic don't realize they are doing it; they just do it as a reaction to what intimidates them. One of the indications that this is what's operating is, the one who commissioned you to do something is the same one going behind your back to sabotage you in that very position. It's insane but it's real. At one ministry I served in, I was the only minstrel that was not on salary. You have to decide what you're going to be. When I was a musician and singer, I was motivated by the envelope I received at the end of my gig. Now, I am motivated by God's promises, where I get into His presence and get what I need.

I understand that a hireling is a hireling. I've been on both sides of the fence. Hirelings don't pay anything to the house. That's stupid to them. Their mentality is, "Why give you 10% of what you owe me?" The fruit of a hireling is they can't sit still. They never stay in the sanctuary for the Word, because they have none in them. They're usually gone when the preacher is done preaching, to get to the next service. They can't be covenantal. Doesn't the Bible say the sower sows the Word (Mark 4:14)?

I've had people ask me to give them lessons. I'm not a musician. Musician's give lessons. Minstrels give impartations. I can't teach you how to play, but I can supernaturally impart the grace to play. When I received my impartation, at the age of 5 years old, I sat down and tested my impartation. I played one particular song on a 45 record, over and over until I could imitate it. I told God, "If you teach me how to play, I will always give you the glory for it." I recognized I was different. Because of my background of poverty, I never owned my own keyboard. I always had to play someone else's keyboard. I didn't own my own keyboard until age 35. Each band I played in (though they preferred me over other keyboardists) put me out of the band because I did not own my own keyboard. I've been rejected all my life. I was even rejected because I didn't know how to read music in these bands. The Spirit of God caused me to play. So, when I played what they were playing without sight-reading ability, they didn't know how to handle me. In church settings, I was fired from positions because I did not know popular songs. Today, I still do not know popular songs. I only know the songs God downloads to me.

Chapter Five
The Role of Psalmists

Psalmists are known by many different names, but we typically label them "praise and worship leaders." Whatever the title, they are typically the same person with the same assignment- to lead a corporate body of believers in worship. The role of a psalmist is the perfect picture of what surfing looks like. The law of surfing is to stay inside of the wave so you don't get killed. You catch the wave; you don't make the wave. When the psalmist steps out of order and attempts to make the wave before the minstrel, it sounds like and creates confusion. Then the minstrel is left searching for where the psalmist is. This is out of order. The problem in our praise and worship service is that we never ask the Lord about the activity going on in Heaven. We start our own services and list of songs, never asking God where Holy Spirit is stirring. It is pivotal to ask to join Heaven's flow, instead of creating your own flow. That's why it takes so long to get into the flow. Minstrels are supposed to just come in and play, waiting on God to shift them to the flow that's taking place in Heaven. This is called tapping into the river that's already flowing. Once this takes place, psalmists come in and interpret vocally what's being played by hand. The hand of a minstrel symbolizes words. When the minstrel is anointed, you can hear the words. The psalmist sings the interpretation. They don't sing out of the flow of the Spirit. In our culture, we don't sit and wait in His presence to hear the flow. Sadly, that's a representation of our personal prayer life. We're always doing the talking, instead of listening. When we're done listing what we need, we're gone. You've got things to do. As a people, we want to control. We say, "Holy Spirit take control," then we take it back. We want Him to take control on our terms, not His.

Myths Concerning Psalmists

There is a myth that plagues psalmists. The myth is that it's the psalmists' role to "take us in." Allow me to set this straight. It is not their role to take you "in" to get your breakthrough. The responsibility lies on Holy Spirit to do this work. Secure a relationship with the Lord at home. If you can't let Holy Spirit guide you in prayer, how are you going to yield to Him doing anything in other people's lives? David was able to do what he did based on his relationship with God, not his skill level. It's all about relationship.

What is highlighted in praise and worship today is all about skill. People sharpen skill, not character, behind closed doors. Because of the nature of the audience, people can get away with not having character. They want to be entertained by how good you are. Churches recruit based on the highest skill level and talent. They want them to sound perfect for *them*, not God. In essence, the church has been bamboozled with confusing what sounds good, with what is anointed. One doesn't have anything to do with the other. What psalmists do on stage should be an extension of what they do at home in their personal relationship with God. They shouldn't be two different people. We see the opposite, all the time. Most people can't do what they do on stage, at home. They have no people to do it in front of. In essence, they're being motivated by the crowd, not the cloud.

Equally, the congregation has a responsibility to have a relationship with God's spirit. The worship leader should not be the only person in corporate worship with a relationship to God's Spirit. Instead of critiquing the worship taking place because it isn't your favorite, get on one-accord and unified with the minstrels and psalmists to worship God. You may be asking, "How can we all sincerely get on one-accord? "What if the person isn't saved?" If everyone saved is on one-accord and love is flowing, the Bible says everyone will be drawn and respond to the love they see (John 13:35). We can genuinely all respond to Holy Spirit.

Another myth claims that the worship leader is supposed to be someone who is charismatic and hype. We want people to hype us as if we're at a show or concert. Unrealistic expectation also claims they have to take us somewhere. The only responsibility is that they are required to go where everyone else is supposed to go. Again, if the worship leader isn't going anywhere, how can they lead the congregation? Psalmists, sing the song and stop being a narrator. Don't give instructions and hype people. This is why worship leaders have jacked up lives. They are trying to do more than they are supposed to. You're out of your jurisdiction if you're trying to embody the minstrel and Holy Spirit. You're trying to create the flow, take the people in, and take credit for doing it successfully. What is a true success to us, may not even be the success that God was trying to accomplish. Getting our flesh pleased is not a success. Success is getting lives changed because of their encounter with God's presence. We are tasked with creating a spiritual climate where Jesus can come in the midst of us. When this happens, no one will leave the same way they came. This is why the worship leader shouldn't do it all. We are a body that is gifted to work in harmony together. You're worn out because you won't let anybody do anything. What's the point in having a praise team, if the worship leader is doing everything? This is the inclination of a lead singer for a band. A worship leader doesn't have to stand out front with a microphone. Why don't you stand together? You need that DIVA demon cast out of you if you're trying to be seen.

The Holy Spirit does the changing, not us. Additionally, God set up support through the gift and support of a minstrel. Every declaration made in Psalms was accompanied by a minstrel. God knew the use of the minstrel is protection for your body. He put the evil spirit in Saul, to create the opportunity to use a minstrel. He used David, which was the only man that he addressed was after his own heart. Why is that? It didn't have anything to do with David's life, mistakes, or sins, but the fact that David would obey him at any cost. Simple obedience at all cost, this is real worship. This is the dynamic missing in our church.

Despite the mistakes of an individual, leaders have no right to tell the minstrel and psalmist to follow Holy Spirit, but then you flip the script, wanting them to follow you. You're teaching them obedience to you, but disobedience to God. You have them confused with loyalty to man versus obedience to God. That is pure confusion. By nature, we tend to reject something that's foreign to us. We have an erroneous myth out that leaders can't be corrected. That's not even biblical. So because you have a title, the Word doesn't apply to you? Your title doesn't excuse you from the Word. You can't beat your members and staff with the Word, and then reject the Word for yourself. It doesn't work that way. As a leader and apostle, I know that I am subject to the Word before I can expect anyone else to be.

Psalmists, check the posture of your heart. What's motivating you? Why do you feel it's your responsibility to move the crowd? Stick to allowing Holy Spirit to lead you. Don't make adjustments to appease the crowd, because that's what will cause you to get off. Release what you hear, even if the crowd says nothing. You need to stay focused on what God told you to do, knowing you will get Him the end result. Some psalmists don't even ask God what He wants to hear because they're worried about what people want to hear. People are fickle. You will always deviate from what God wants when looking at the face of the people. You will always fall into what the people want. This is the spirit of Saul. Saul was the people's choice, but David was God's choice. As soon as you disobey God, people are on to the next person. The psalmist was created to bring God glory, not the people. Often, our leaders are so busy trying to please people that they fail to focus on pleasing God. The church is user-friendly for people, but not God-accessible. We prepare more for the guest speaker to come than the King of Kings and Lord of Lord's. We prepare for a man or woman with 2-3 published books, to grace our stage. There is something wrong with this. We aren't even loyal. We miss services until our favorite person comes to preach. God is raising up something RAW (Real Authentic Worshipers). You will be disappointed with these raw worshipers coming up because their worship is not for you. For them, it's always been for the King of Kings, anyway.

I'm exposing this because of the unlearned. They don't want to deal with the agenda conflicts involving the real issue. Sadly, the real issue is that worship is not important to leaders today. Leaders reject anything that interrupts their cash flow. They realize that a standard of holiness will cause a lot of people not to come around. You cannot have a mega-mess and holiness at the same time.

Honor in Judah

Something that happens a lot in Judah is that people get their position or role based on the backs of others. You should never do this to get what you want. What you sow, you'll definitely reap. It's a dangerous place to discredit someone before you to get your position. Down through the years, I've seen leaders complain about the worship leader to the Pastor, in hopes of getting the position. When you're given the position, after discrediting the previous person, you're out of order. You'll discover you don't get cooperation from the team now because you've sown the seed of discredit. You will reap what you've sown. This comes from how we've been conditioned in the church world.

Instead of participating in worship, the entire team is critiquing. We compare what we are impressed with versus what God has blessed us with. We want our team to sound like who we are impressed with. Then we force them to fit the standard we want to hear and critique it because we want to hear that. God may love what your worship team is giving. Our love level is so low that we are unable to love the gifts God has blessed our lives with. In essence, we're telling God, "I don't appreciate the gifts you've sent us." We are saying we want someone more talented and someone that makes us feel good enough to appease our flesh. We don't want purity; we want talent. We want the church that has the better band and singers. We label it "a desire to operate in the spirit of excellence." That's not true. What we really want is to compete with the other church to ensure that we have the best of the best. You don't want the person that only knows two chords and loves God. Why is our church holding auditions instead of interviews? Interviews tell you the condition of the heart. Auditions are worldly. The condition of the heart produces the sound God is looking for. Your pastor is looking for who sounds the best and is most talented. That's why our churches have the highest turnover rate because the church is trying to pull the best MD (music director) to produce the sound you want. We will pay any price to compete and get the best in our church. Yet, the person with a good heart, you won't even give them a chance. In essence, we are no better than the world. "A spirit of excellence" is not even scriptural. We adopt worldly concepts to address what we want.

When I gathered a praise team, I used all the misfit worshipers. I gathered people who had a reputation for being a troublemaker, less talented, and rejected, on purpose. Church administration disallowed me from targeting the best of the best. I was told that I couldn't use anybody from the other praise teams. Yet, my goal was never to use them anyway. They thought they were setting me up to fail. They didn't know that those targeted people were more like Jesus. We had a different sound than any other team. Their talent was subpar, but their sound was perfect, because of their hearts. A lot of them weren't considered singers. I didn't want singers; I wanted worshipers. I used to bring them to my house, cook for them and fellowship with them. We got to know each other, outside of the church and didn't talk about anything church-related. You find out who people are when you bring them in a setting where they can be themselves. The purpose of having fellowship with people you're ministering with is when the spirit of division comes to disrupt your unity, you already know the character of that person through fellowship- so you don't take the attack out on them by getting offended. If you know them by the spirit (because you've fellowshipped), you'll attack the spirit of division attacking them, because you know the true nature of the person laboring among you. When our team worshipped, we gave the crowd an extension of our love and fellowship together. We didn't give anything fake. I didn't require the minstrels to learn songs, I required them to live holy. When we came together to worship, Holy Spirit orchestrated our sound.

This is why I waited so long to release this book. Everyone I shared these revelations with tried to write something before I did. I wasn't worried about it, because, they can write it, but they can't live it. I've already lived out these chapters. I never decided to be an apostle of divine arts, I discovered it after doing the work. The apostle of divine arts chose me; I didn't choose it. After being raised a PK (preacher's kid), I didn't even want to be a minister.

To the worship leader and psalmist, if people don't get with you, what difference does it make? Your corporate worship time should be an extension of your private worship time at home. The congregation isn't home with you when you're worshipping. So, there is no difference. What difference does it make if they don't get with you corporately? People should see your relationship, not your talent. The fact that you care and it bothers you when they don't get with you is a setup from the enemy. The purpose of the setup is to get you to operate like him. Lucifer still wants to be like God. He wants to set you up to take the responsibility that only belongs to God. That's way above your pay grade. That's the spirit of Lucifer rising up. If you've ever heard or said, "I'm gon' take 'em somewhere today," that's the spirit I'm referring to. No, that person needs to sit out and get out of the way. If they were smart, they would get out of the way and allow God to deal with their heart.

To the worship leader that has been taken down, because of the preferences of men, just know that you were blamed for something that was never your responsibility in the first place. It's easier for the pastor to be suspicious of you being to blame, than for them to take responsibility for their ignorance. When the worship doesn't go right, the pastor will blame you. The worship leader is often set up for the fall. The ignorance comes from the church's lack of understanding concerning their responsibilities in corporate worship. It is a corporate and unified responsibility, not just the praise team and worship leader's responsibility. We bring other specialists in to teach all this other fluff: kingdom, prophetic, dreams, finances, etc. However, we won't bring in a specialist to teach about worship. We fail to prepare people to function in the Heavens as if we won't be going. Yet, we prepare them for conferences. All we will do is worship 24/7, for eternity.

God Wants Pure Worship

The first shall be last and the last shall be first. The purity of worship was the last thing on the church's agenda. God is bringing it to the forefront because this is what He wants. When you are called to worship arts, you face battles totally different from the average believer. The persecution is to squeeze pure worship out of you. Until you get to the place that you will give God pure worship, despite your circumstance, you will face persecution. God is cashing in on His investment in you. Think about all the years you were just getting by. Some things God doesn't just give us because He wants more worship. With more time comes more worship. God knows what's coming ahead and what you need to sustain you.

There is a myth I'd like to address concerning bringing God the sacrifice of praise. If you're in a country where you're forbidden from worshiping God, you know the sacrifice you face if you're caught. That's the epitome of sacrifice. This sacrifice of praise we sing and talk about living in the United States of America is a joke compared to what some of the Body experiences. Some of us won't sacrifice sleep to get out of the bed to go to corporate worship. If we make it, we have to be bribed to lift our hands and participate.

Choosing Worship Leaders

I need to expose the error that takes place in choosing worship leaders. Often, pastors choose people that accommodate their needs, not God's. They choose someone they can control. Most of all, they don't choose someone who can take them where God wants them to go. This is a huge danger. People who have a Davidic oil on their lives are rejected. They can't help themselves. They aren't trying to please people. They are just seeking the heart of the Father. Yes, they *are* defiant, but it's understandable, as they would rather obey God than obey you.

For years, because of the anointing on my life, I was called a renegade. Because the anointed shifted atmospheres, leaders said I dabbled in witchcraft and was a warlock. That's the fruit of Jesus because anything that is truly of God is usually rejected as Christ was. Remember, the Pharisees accused Jesus healing by the work of Beelzebub (Luke 11:15). If the results scare you, you need to take it up with God. I was warned by the Father that if I was anything like Jesus or David, I would be despised and should not act surprised.

DAVIDIC REFORMATION

Chapter Six
The David and Saul Dynamic

David loved Saul greatly and refused to touch him, even after Saul made several attempts against David's life. Leaders that operate in this system always have an excuse for why they treat the David's in their life a certain way. They feel and say things like, "They get paid more than me, they don't do as much work as I do." They make excuses why they treat Judah the way they do. The reason they make excuses is that they don't want to admit they are wrong. Even with writing this book and my assignment to point out what's wrong, there will be someone accusing me of being negative. Understand that I've been on both sides of the spectrum. I have been a minister and then progressed to become an apostle- which proves my validity. I lived all the experiences I have mentioned and then put them in this book. I have been on both sides of the fence. When I speak against something to restore order in that area, it is because God corrected me in that area and tasked me with the assignment to bring revelation to the Body. We have a responsibility to get our instruction from God. If we all got our designs from God, they wouldn't necessarily look similar, but the results would. Everybody's instructions aren't necessarily the same because He created us diverse. Now, if our results are zero to none, something is missing. The method has to change. This is why reform is so important. Leaders this is also why you are obligated to use your authority with care. You could cause delay and pain in people when all you had to do was take it to God instead of opening your mouth against people you don't understand. The Saul system covers up flaws, and it's rooted in disobedience. God's unctioning you to put honor on the least of them, but you only want to put honor on those that please you. Davidic people put honor where honor is due, not the one that caters to you. The system of Saul puts honor on people they like. Sadly, if leaders don't like you, you're not getting honor. I believe honor should be based on your merit and increase, not popularity. Again, the Saul system works on people's choice, not God's choice. I've heard people say, "I like him; he always has something nice to say." However, the one who comes with correction, nobody likes them and tries to shut them up and shut them down.

Crooked leadership leads to places of distortion and systems that are off from God's frequency. Don't allow a crooked system to knock you off the square that God has ordained you to dominate.

What you'll need to do is change your focus. Remember that praise and worship are for Him, not you. The pain and blessing of being rejected by people can cause you to focus on the purpose for which you are doing what you're doing. Rejection comes with the assignment to destroy your passion and your drive for doing what God called you to do. Anything God wants to say, He can say through the song. That's why He wants a new song. He's trying to get His voice heard, which is why prophetic worship is so important. In a true prophetic house, you'll find, God is usually not using what you've studied for your sermon. You're giving people what you know, not what they need. The same applies to Judah. We need to be singing to release what people need, not what we know. When you sing the same popular song it releases the same redundant manna. However, a new song draws on time you've spent with Him through the week. He breathes afresh. But when you give Him only what you want to hear, you only hear yourself. It's bad enough that you only give Him a limited frame of time to be heard anyway.

The System of Saul

This system of Saul is usually the picture of how the majority of how our churches are set up. Saul was the people's choice. So, if your church is based on a Saul system, the people are getting what they want, not what God is requiring. The choir or praise team sings songs they or the pastor like. That's a Saul system. In fact, that pastor was probably voted in because that's what the people wanted. When the people vote you in, they can also vote you out, when you don't do what they want. The pastor controlled by a Saul system will not allow certain sermons to be preached. They will preach what makes the people happy- not addressing certain sins and definitely not bring up holiness. He or she does not want to insult the people who give the most. This leader does what he or she has to do to make the people happy, but not effective. Saul only represented 1000 victories. David, on the other hand, represented tens of thousands of victories. David did not care if something was not of God; he killed it. David was never the people's choice; he was God's choice. That was proven with him being anointed as king. Samuel came seeking out the new king, looking through his brothers (I Samuel 16:1-11). In these days, Jesse's sons would have been the people that went through all the necessary classes to be elevated in our church. Yet,

Um? kinda but also God's.

Samuel said these all look good, but there must be another. Our churches seek out people in the same manner. We seek out those that look good. We don't seek out those who God's hand is upon.

The church is happy with only 1000 victories. It refuses to get away from the Saul system in place and allow the Davidic order to come in.

The Saul system is a place of disobedience. The Davidic system represents obedience. David would not allow the enemy to have anything on him because he told on himself. We see countless times in the Word where David got in the face of God and repented and lamented in agony concerning his weaknesses and shortcomings. Everything he did was sparked by obedience from God. In a lot of instances, he took up for God and wouldn't allow people to take offense with his God. Saul system doesn't show relationship with God. That's why you can get up there and sing any kind of song and live any kind of way, but you reflect no relationship with God.

A Saul driven environment doesn't drive you to live any disciplined lifestyle. It allows you to live any way you want. I'm sure leaders operating in a Saul system will not appreciate the exposing of darkness behind these systems and defend their Saul nature, but it's self-explanatory. If you're going to continue to follow a leader defending and perpetuating a system that tried to kill David because of jealousy, that's on you. When you live the live comparison of Saul and David, there is no comparison. I would rather live victoriously like David did.

God had to break me to show me that I wasn't all that. He broke my character and no matter what leaders did to me; I didn't change the way I treated them, in retaliation. I honored them and allowed God to defend me so that He could promote me in due time. God increased my love level so I couldn't feel the injustice when it was happening to me. He showed me the model of honor in the life of David when Saul tried to kill him. Saul threw javelins and even when David had the advantage and could have killed Saul, he wouldn't. He loved Saul greatly. I had to walk with leaders who destroyed my name through the false reproaches they put on me. The myth has been that when people talk about you, it shouldn't affect you if God is with you. That's a lie because a lie has no power except it is told by someone with authority. That's why as a leader, what you say out of your mouth is a responsibility, not an opportunity.

We are all a body. We all have to be careful what we say about our body. The rest of the body will respond. If someone with authority speaks a lie about you, who do you think they'll believe- you or someone that has a couple books out? People are not faithful as God is. They are downright cruel. They will support you as long as they know nothing about you. If they hear a rumor about you they will jump on it- choosing not to use discernment. Based on who said it, they will believe it. How many times have we heard, "Who said it...oh yeah, it had to be true!" So, then you have to suffer until God vindicates you of the false reproach on your name. We don't automatically see the fruit of what was said about us. You have to wait awhile and God will vindicate you. I know what I'm talking about. I lived through it. As much as I sowed into the Kingdom, I should never be in a place of comeback. But, low and behold, that's where I am. I am not surprised though. Why? My life has been in a Davidic pattern in a Saul system. Javelins have been thrown at me, constantly. It has nothing to do with what I did. It's because of who I was. There is no reason for people not to place proper honor on you unless they did not know who you were.

This David/Saul dynamic has ruined a lot of lives. It keeps jealousy prevalent in Davidic people. Saul refused to place honor on David because he was jealous of him and was afraid David would supersede him. Which is twisted, because if your children don't supersede you, you're not really apostolic. Of all the things Jesus spoke, he left us with "greater works" will we do than Him. This is why I know some of you reading this will relate to not being promoted since Jesus was a baby boy. You're told and showed why you are not ready. That's not the heart of God because if you're not released, you won't get ready. For some of you, the devil is not holding you back; your pastor/leader is. He or she is holding you back to keep themselves looking good. Saul held David back because he was afraid of him making him look bad. Touch your neighbor and say, "Davidic reformation."

The results David and Saul got speak for itself. When you have a Davidic presence in your church it helps the church to flourish. The people flourish as well- not just the set man. Saul was appointed by people. David was appointed by God. David was a great example of being an apostle. He was out doing the work of a shepherd when Samuel was looking for him, to anoint him as king. He was occupying until God came. Saul was looking to be noticed and chosen by the people. You can allow people to put you up and be content with that, but you'll only get 1000 victories. When you allow God to endorse you, people discover who you are after you've done the work. Yet, you'll have tens of thousands of victories- which will be continual.

Chapter Seven
Songs of Saul vs. Davidic Songs

The songs of Saul are basically songs of preference-not songs required by God. They are most preferred because everyone is singing them. This has become our learned behavior, to sing what's popular. Singing songs of Saul keeps you locked in parameters of man's control. David's model of prophetic worship expressed freedom. It was not adjacent to a system. Singing Davidic songs open you to realms that are endless and allow God to take over like you prayed and asked for. Davidic songs sing of being victorious because they are sparked by God himself. This proves that praise and worship were for Him in the first place, not us. So, if it's for Him, we should be singing His favorite songs, not ours.

When singing songs of Saul, you shouldn't be surprised that you experience the same results. You shouldn't be surprised that you're not experiencing breakthrough. You certainly should not be surprised that you're only getting 1000 victories. Most songs of Saul come from a familiar place. That place is based on your preference and not a place of seeking God for what He wants. We usually have no connection with God's agenda when we do what we want. This familiar place is manipulated by leaders that are ignorant of the purpose of praise and worship. You think it's just something people do before the preacher gets up to preach their message. So, you sing the same songs everybody is listening to while trying to outdo the other. The only change you hear involves the team making up their own versions. That's the fruit of the song of Saul. It doesn't mean they aren't good or anointed songs. However, they have no place in the gathering of kings who are seeking instructions from the King of Kings on how to change their environments (Revelation 19:16). So, how in the world do you think you are going to change the mountain of influence you are assigned to when you can't change a hill that keeps erecting in your house? It's not going to happen. As the worship team recycles popular songs on their song list, the songs of Saul cause you (in your local setting) to recycle situations, demons, and demonic presence. That's because singing recycled songs limit you to only touching the surface. It doesn't penetrate, to evoke change. Witches, warlocks, and rebellious people can comfortably stay in our services and go home because nothing in our services effect change. We sing songs that were created with unclean hands. Most of these people don't have a lifestyle that back up these songs. They will tell you themselves that this is nothing but a job for them. Yet, Davidic songs are sparked by the Spirit of God and spark change. David changed a whole nation with his worship.

We don't even have to be deep to realize both sides are being affected. Most songs we hear today are keeping crime alive and our communities tainted. Yet, we will endorse that faster than we will something pure, because we've been programmed that it has to move our flesh. The same thing happens in church. If it doesn't move your flesh you won't participate. Yet, you have no problem critiquing or criticizing it. You don't critique or criticize the world's music. I know more people who have bought Beyoncé than Michael W. Smith. Then they want to be like Beyoncé. You want to be a diva? Then you dress like the people in the videos your children are watching. On top of that, you'll give your money to Beyoncé and Jay-Z, but you don't even want to pay for a conference to get prayed for. You will go to a concert and pay $12 for a hot dog and won't complain about it. To top it off, you'll holler during the entire concert. In church they have to pay you to lift your hands to participate. Our priorities are twisted. We've been programmed to adapt to the Saul system and we've been bamboozled.

The mindset is, "Let's get a good idea," not a God-idea. We use this excuse to pursue our own preferences. If you were dependent on the creator to create something, you wouldn't use something corrupt to get your point across. I don't need the devil to get my point across. That mindset says two things: 1) You're not spending time with God to get anything fresh and, 2) You're using ungodly music to target audiences- making them connect with a point in time when they were in sin. The question has been often asked about musicians that wander in church and play or use secular songs from the past to make a Gospel song by changing some of the lyrics. Musically, it's the same song, and yes, it is still contaminated. People who use that technique show they are not getting in the face of God. That is the tell-tell sign. God will always give you something new. There is nothing known as writers' block when you get in the face of the writer. Holy Spirit never runs out; we do.

Some of the top Gospel artists are frauds. They achieve success by standing on the back of secular music. Music carries a lot of weight. Those secular songs had time-zones and particular sins attached to them. You should not be singing songs that remind you of a time when you were not godly. You weren't safe, let alone saved. Is that what you offer up to a holy God? I don't think so. Now, it's okay if your only goal was to sell albums to make money. That's all you're going to accomplish, anyway. Producing music like that, you're telling the world, we want to be like you- not we want you to be like us. What have we been offering the King?

We offer Him what we want and not what He's requiring. It's difficult to know what He wants when you don't ask. I ask what He wants to hear and where Heaven is flowing right now. We miss it because we've been programmed to come out with a praise song first. Fast or slow does not depict praise or worship. The difference is related to the content you are singing, not the tempo.

The reason for the exposure is to stop us from producing boys disguised as men and girls disguised as women, behind pulpits. In addition, we must stop producing dysfunctional worship leaders who are directly produced through dysfunctional systems. We blame the dysfunction on what we hear from worship leaders, but we're actually reaping the dysfunction we've sown. Leaders who have nothing to do with the music department are even affected by this dysfunction. They get impartations through the frequencies of dysfunction released in the atmosphere. So, we're producing unhealthy leaders who go out and reproduce unhealthy leaders. It's a cycle of dysfunction. The enemy has used the divide and conquer strategy for years. You even see leaders separating themselves-unable to have a relationship with other leaders. If you read the Bible correctly, the prophets benefited and were changed and elevated when they came in contact with Davidic anointing and minstrels. The Saul system keeps the ministry gifts separated. Judah has been separated from the other ministry gifts. It is the only ministry gift that attends conferences on worship. Aren't we all worshipers? Everyone needs to know how to conduct themselves in corporate worship. Everyone needs to know how to place a demand on what they need out of worship.

I've seen disrespect from the prophetic team during worship. We don't want to hear that the spirit of the prophet is subject to the prophet. What do you think minstrels are? They're prophets. What do you think they're doing with their hands? They are prophesying. I've lived through all I'm saying. If you have more confidence in the status of your leader than you do confidence in God, you've already lost. That's the danger in thinking you are more than you are. The fruit of that is you can never be corrected. Leaders tend to always think you have to be made to honor and respect them, instead of the fruit they produce. It's difficult for me to respect you when you make me respect and honor you. You're requiring honor for yourself, and it doesn't work like that.

The System of Jezebel

People who dabble in a Jezebelic system will always seek to control and shut down pure worship. I was often shut down, by people who flowed in the spirit of Jezebel. They would not allow me to play behind them. Other ministry gifts accused me of taking over entire services when I played. These rumors, when spread, made people skeptical and afraid of me. In several settings, I had no clue these lies were being spread. This caused me to live for years under a false reproach against my name. I learned to keep my face in the face of God and He allowed me to produce godly results. You don't have to clear your name. God will vindicate when you belong to Him. God told me that sometimes you have to agree with your adversary. They were right; when I played, there was something different. I was on God's frequency, so of course, it was true that they'd never heard the frequency He was releasing. When they release these lies, it's important to keep doing what God instructs you to do. The only person that will come up looking bad is those releasing false reproach against your name. Obedience will not cause you to look bad, and certainly, God will not either. Our way is not the way, God's way is the way.

good things bear fruit.

DAVIDIC REFORMATION

Chapter Eight
The Forbidden Instrument

The only instrument that has no biblical reference to David is the organ. The earliest mention of the organ was in the 3rd Century (285-222 BC) which had no correlation to ancient Israel. The organ's first known manipulation and correlation was to the arenas of the Roman Empire, where it was played during races and games. The early Church of Rome came down against organs, disallowing them from being used. Rome's last known emperor, Nero (who was known for his fits of rage), blamed Rome's great burning on Christians and after having them captured and burned alive, played the organ while listening to them scream. That's why the only places where the organ remains today is in dead churches, funeral homes, and baseball parks. Anywhere it remains there is a strong influence of perversion because it's original sound and definition have been perverted. To pervert something is to change the inherent purpose or function of it. The original description of what Bible translators were trying to connect to an organ was correctly translated as pipes. Strong's dictionary defines the root Hebrew word for organ as 'uwgab, in its original meaning, as a sense of breathing or blowing. Its proper definition is a musical instrument in the form of a flute, reed-pipe, or panpipe. God gave David the technology to hollow out logs and hang them on a tree so God could breathe through them to make a sound. The sound of pipes and the breath and sound of God was never meant to be trapped in a box. When man puts their hands on it, it perverts it. When you hear the sound of an organ, it's aggravated and perverts the sound of God. This is why in a church service, when the organ stops playing, the people will stop dancing once whatever spirit came in leaves. The organ is used to spark an emotion because most congregations are sparked by emotion. That's why they are used in funeral homes. They spark up thoughts of the past. They will never create a new sound. This instrument was around for more than 1100 years, in the secular arena and circus, before it made its way into a church setting.[2]

Those of you who have adopted it as a sacred cow need to know that an organ is one-dimensional. It can only access one realm- the realm it was created to

---

[2] End of chapter references

produce. It was created to reproduce after its own kind. It's an instrument of perversion. Therefore, it reproduces perversion. There is power in what you name a thing. Symbolically, people should not be perverting, playing, or playing *with* an "organ." That's why homosexuality can remain in a place where that sound is played. Jezebel can operate in that atmosphere with no hindrances. Witches can operate wherever that sound is prevalent. The old time way is still around as long as that sound is prevalent and dominant. Sickness, sin, and disease are always around when that sound is prevalent and dominant. It doesn't help when the person playing it is still in sin. Whatever is in the person, when the instrument is being played, it is going through the speaker. Music and frequencies are the only things that don't need permission to enter your spirit. The radio has been raping us for years- pumping frequencies into our spirits. It's been a known fact that gifts and callings come without repentance (Romans 11:29).

I've seen Gospel artists that were apostles but didn't know it. So everyone who played like them got an impartation from them. Everyone who was a part of their life got an impartation from them, because of what was in them. As a result, those same Gospel artists died from AIDS and so did several of their "sons."

I often see minstrels try to make a transition from the organ to the keyboard because they got a revelation about it. However, they set the keyboard on top of the organ because they can't get away from it. That's how powerful the darkness is in it. A lot of people will argue with me about the forbidden instrument. Yet, look at the lives of those arguing this point. The minstrel who insists on playing the organ will exemplify the same characteristics of the sound the organ produces: nothing fresh, unable to tap into the new, and unable to access new and fresh realms. We often gravitate toward what's comfortable for our flesh. Anything that is new often creates a challenge to change. That makes any flesh uncomfortable. I've had many leaders tell me, "I like my Hammond B3," and I respond, "Make sure you like everything that comes with that Hammond B3." As an apostle of divine arts, God has heightened my sensitivity to sound. When I am invited to minister to a place, it's usually only one time. I'm challenged with addressing the leader with their challenge with Jezebel. If I hear that sound, I know that church is plagued with teen pregnancy, infidelity, adultery, homosexuality, and a long, long line of counseling. It doesn't help that many of the things that sound created have been legalized, which makes those sins more flamboyant now. What am I saying? The organ has no place.

Stringed instruments like the guitar and bass are referenced in Davidic worship. Psalms records, "I will incline my ear to a parable: I will disclose my dark saying upon the harp" and "I will sing a new song to You, O God; On a harp of ten strings I will sing praises to You" (Psalms 49:4, 144:9). Psalms' specificity in describing the instruments is meant to kill the argument that they should not be used in worship. The mention of using 10 strings was very specific. There are 6 strings on a lead guitar and 4 on bass guitar. There are your ten strings. Sidebar: I just believe the Bible is not a menu where you can pick and choose what you want to partake of or not. Drums are timbres and cymbals; that's a drum set. Many people will argue and say drums shouldn't be loud in worship. Yet, that's ignorant. What does Psalms 150 command us to do? The organ is the only instrument that should be forbidden because of its origin and manipulation of function. They are in dead churches that don't have God visit them anymore, and they don't even realize it. He doesn't come because you don't need Him and you've got it under control.

The keyboard and piano are mentioned in Davidic worship. The piano is nothing but a harp in a box. A modified version of a piano is a lute. David couldn't march with a piano, so he modified it and put it on a stick to march with and be played. The keyboard is universal. It was modified by man, but not perverted. It was modified to access different sounds and realms. It allows Holy Spirit to help you access different realms.

The Saul system made it very difficult for the common man to tell what sounds good versus what's anointed. The anointing never gets stale, because it's born of the Spirit and has no shelf life. Yet, when something is created out of a familiar place or has no anointing on it, it becomes annoying and it fades away. God has never required us to stay current and cutting edge. He's required for us to worship Him in Spirit and truth and stay obedient. If you stay obedient, you'll stay current. One of the ways of knowing if your church is catering to the flesh is when you choose things that satisfy you, and your decision is based on your preference as opposed to what's required by God. We will not see reform if we choose to be in denial of what we're doing wrong. Holiness has become a subject or topic and not a way of life. I realize a lot of our problems are not complicated to solve. We just need to admit and rebuild with the right foundation- not any old foundation. As long as we're in denial, the churches theme song will always be "This is How We Do It." For the older generation, their theme song will be, "I Did It My Way." For the millennials, it will be, "You've Lost That Lovin' feeling." I am not picking on Judah because I did the same thing. I've been on both sides, but God delivered me. I want to make sure you, the reader, know I am not pointing the finger at you. I am a part of the Body of Christ. I feel I can expose it because I've done it.

---

2 Additional references concerning the organ:

http://strangeside.com/shuls-the-organ-controversy/
https://www.die-orgelseite.de/historie_e.htm

DAVIDIC REFORMATION

https://jhva.wordpress.com/tag/magrefa/
http://www.westfield.org/programs/curious-facts/
http://www.jewishencyclopedia.com/articles/11761-
organ

DAVIDIC REFORMATION

Chapter Nine
Favorites

There is a great lack of honor in the music department. Leaders are bad about having their favorites. I've seen leaders who listened more to their families than God. In a Jezebel system, you want people you can control and who are put in control, so you can manipulate everything in the house. It disguises itself as loyalty, but it's loyalty to man- not faithfulness to God. Anytime you have a leader who will systematically destroy you when you disagree with them, that is a Saul/David dynamic. The system of Saul seeks to destroy you when you challenge them. You should be able to respectfully disagree with someone without them seeking to destroy you. When you put me between obedience to you and disobedience to God, you'll lose every time. I don't allow grey areas. You can't make me agree with you. I must obey God. This is why I've been called a renegade and disagreeable.

"Rebellious" is not a nickname for someone that you can't control; neither is "renegade" a nickname for someone that doesn't agree with you. We have to be careful as leaders about being so quick to be offended, and out of that offense, label people. These labels make life in ministry hard for people. Then they are blamed for it. That goes especially for individuals who are creative in the arts and creative in all forms of music. They were never designed to be corralled like horses. If you remember in Scripture, when they came to find the king out of the house of Jesse, all of his sons were in the house where they were corralled and shown like prize horses. Yet, David was out back with the sheep. He was free. Big difference! We need more David's to step up, obey, and defend the things of God.

We do so many things in the Lord's house that should not be allowed. David went as far as to modify instruments that were not holy enough for God. This is why God chose someone who wasn't afraid to stand up to leaders to defend the things of God. The characteristic of being Davidic is the devil can never have anything on you because you've told God everything. The devil can never tell God anything about me because Jacques told God everything already. God was already there, watching me do it. This is the thing that kept David so pure before God.

124

Dismantling Man-Made Structures

Judah has to be cleaned up first. Therefore, it must start with the leadership. It must start with how Judah is treated. The budget must be released some. It shouldn't always be used to buy Hummers and to fly first class on these elaborate trips. It won't kill you to fly coach when I can still see you eight rows ahead of me. Now, we can travel and do all of these things, when we spend our own money. However, leaders are spending the money set aside for ministry. This is the money of those who are still sitting at home. We cannot step on the backs of the people of God to elevate ourselves higher than them. You're flying and living in luxury, but your music department (that you use on a regular basis) is in ruins. This department has allowed you to access realms that you could never access yourself, but you'll never admit that. Something is wrong with that picture. Some of the most glorious experiences I've had was when the psalmist and minstrels got on one accord, and the pastor was not around. When the leader's hands are not on it, there is a freedom on the worship. We don't need to be navigated by man; we need to be free to be navigated by Holy Spirit. Even the nature of God and Jesus is opposed to this. They don't give you directions or instructions to control you. They give you God's commandments and the freedom of choice, but tell you which one you should choose. Because God is covenantal, He always explains the benefits of choosing the right thing and the consequences for choosing the wrong things. This tells me that the church structures in place do not match the heart of God. They are founded on man's structure, which has rendered us powerless. They are rendered by preference. We choose people we prefer because they will do what we tell them to do. We don't want people who will do what God tells them to do because we feel like this is "our church." No, this is God's church. If there was a theme song assigned to the state of today's church, it would be, "This is How We Do It." In my travels, I've gone into churches and I've heard, "This is how we do it. "If you don't convert into this, we'll kill you. Convert to this or die. We will not deviate." Those churches usually don't even know that God doesn't come there anymore. It makes no difference the denomination when you program God out of your gatherings, He'll allow you to keep doing it. There are some things in the apostolic and prophetic movements that have become religious in their own right. Once they experience breakthrough in one area, they won't allow breakthrough in others; that's religious.

So basically, your morals should always remain consistent, but your methods have to change (or be flexible to change). I said it earlier, The Old Ship of Zion is not going to work for Pookie. These are high-tech demons we are dealing with when it comes to young people. Millennials don't believe anything, without evidence. "The sweet by and by" won't work for them. They need right now faith and evidence. Before you approach them with it, you better believe it yourself.

You can't have one system in place for all people that come through your church doors. The world is smart enough to have placement tests to see where people are when they come in the doors. The norm today is to have new members' class for all people- even those who have been through as many years of church training as a senior military soldier has been serving in Afghanistan. We need different placement and programs for the diversity of people coming in. We need better programs that mobilize people who are taking your classes and still dying. People are sitting in your seats watching your favorite teams. What are you doing with the praise teams you won't use because they aren't your favorite? Send those praise teams out to minister in college campuses, coffee houses, etc. I use to train my praise team by having fellowships. I mentioned earlier how I brought them to my home, cooked for them, and got to know them through fellowship with them. I would take them to convalescent and nursing homes- places no one was screaming their name. It taught them to stay focused on God, and not the audience. They learned who they were really doing this for. I trained them as ministers, not entertainers. I trained them to minister while we were worshiping. I trained them to go out in the congregation and share the prophetic word God gave them to share with a person, while we worshiped.

We wonder why we have different spirits coming out of those speakers. We have disgruntled singers and minstrels. People who are serving relentlessly, but are not being supported or sowed back into. I'd rather be serving on the streets of Chicago and playing for people who are not paying me. At least on the streets, people are saying thank you, acknowledging you, and sharing how your music moved them. I would much rather that than to give all my time in a church, where the pastor is escorted to the back before service ends because He is too important to greet those who serve him. Then some of the leaders have the nerve to say, "I'm paying you." But, what you are paying me is just a tip. You are paying me 20% of my time, but I give you 80% of my time. What if the same measurements were applied to you? You're living off our sacrifices but talk to us crazy. This will not take place on my watch. The foolishness has to stop. The way the people who serve are treated has to stop. It's ludicrous for your leaders to come through the back and have the best parking, and are only carrying a bible- all so they can look good on social media. Minstrels have to park two blocks away and carry instruments. That's dishonor. The money is misappropriated. So much is spent on the pastor's security. If someone wanted to get you, all they have to do is go to your favorite restaurant. All they'd have to do is stake out Cracker Barrel. If God can't protect you, your security is doing nothing. If you're living righteous, why do you need an entourage to protect you? Something is wrong.

This is why I mentioned earlier that we need interviews not auditions. When you talk, and get the heart and mind of a person, out of the abundance of the heart, the mouth speaks (Luke 6:45). If you want the right answers, you ask the right questions. I live in the supernatural, because I believe, if the person has the right heart, God can impart the talent for His agenda. We don't want to compensate the right heart; we want to compensate the right chops because they make us look good. Honestly, it doesn't make God look good. We are selfish. We want to cater to ourselves, not satisfy God's agenda. Unfortunately, we are training people to be like us, not Christ. All we hear is, "My Pastor...my pastor a good pastor...my pastor got this and that." How do you think he got it? You gave the money for them to have it. When your lights are getting cut off they will tell you, "We don't have the budget for..." That's because you spent it on you.

When the music department is treated with dishonor, and the title and offerings are misappropriated, there will always be trouble in the finances. The tithes and offerings are not for the pastor to have snakeskin shoes. Davidic order causes everyone in the church to have snakeskin shoes. Davidic reformation ensures that everyone has what they need. How can you lend to nations when you can't even have enough supply for those that serve? That doesn't make sense. Greedy people don't think about supplying for everybody. I'm seeing God raise up David's in this hour that already have what you're dangling in their face, to manipulate them. They will come with it already. They will come with spoils already. They will come with experience to go get what they need from God. This will be abolished while I am alive. God is just.

Because we're on the wrong frequency, we fall for what the media has to offer. That's the wrong frequency that makes us deal with each other dishonorably. It causes the by-product of racial injustice and prejudice. We have more of that in the church than the world now. When we're on the world's frequency, we mimic them more than they mimic the church. The church is progressively mimicking the world. We have nothing to offer the church because we're on the wrong frequency and unexcited about the things of God. How can we expect the world to want to be like us? There are more people in the body of Christ that know more about Jay-Z and the Kardashians than those they worship with every Sunday? If that's the case, I know for sure you aren't praying for them. Then we're unfair to them because if they don't appease our flesh, we don't support them. If they don't measure up, we refuse to support them. I've been making CDs since 1995. I've had to give more away than I sell because people don't know if they'll be impressed or not.

However, we'll go right out and spend money on a CD from someone the media says we should be impressed by. That's wrong.

Our churches are unhealthy because we will financially back someone who already has money, but will not back someone who has no money, but something to offer. Some leaders won't back you if you don't have a product because they don't want you to take away from the money they're trying to get from the people. That's greedy. What leaders don't understand is, if you endorse them, *you* look good. When they reach out to someone who will endorse and support them, you label them as rebellious. That's not smart. As a leader, you're training people to be like you- greedy and not like Jesus. People are more effective by what they see you do than what you say. This is why apostolic fathers must be careful. Our children should be able to say, like Christ, "I only do what I see my father do." I shouldn't have to tell my children to pray, worship, minister to the widow, get involved in the worship, or respond to the Spirit of God. "First apostle" meant we have to be the first to do what we're trying to get everybody else to do. This is for the perfecting of the Body, not to get the biggest piece of chicken. We want to be served first. That's demonic and hierarchical. God's not in that mess.

Another area in which we (as the Body of Christ) need reformation is in the handling of money. I don't allow anybody to stop the flow of worship to manipulate people to give in my gatherings. If the pure presence of God doesn't lead people to give, then we're just manipulating them. There should be an exchange. People get what they need in the presence of God and they give freely. God gave me to set offering buckets out, by the chair of my honored guest, Jesus Christ. Every time we had a gathering, the budget was met. The level of purity supplies the need. Even with my Facebook followers, when I have gatherings, we worship for hours and don't have a charge. We minister healing, prophetic, etc. Yet, people would rather go to a conference, pay for a hotel room, hear a sermon, see a celebrity they can't interact with, and pay for all their material. What they hear in the book, they don't even see in the natural lives of the speakers. I don't want the usual suspects anymore. I would rather go into the streets and get people saved so they can come to the gatherings.

We don't even know how to support our own. When the secular arena picks up some of our psalmists and minstrels and supports their gifts, we call that compromise. I've had people bring a dry spirit to the gatherings- spectating and criticizing, instead of participating. Then, they wonder why the supernatural doesn't happen until they leave. What part of the glory cloud do you bring with you? You're the one heavy because you have 1000 books on the glory, but you're not walking in it. I pray that your eyes would be opened to see that you are your own hindrance. You can't

decipher the anointing because there's none on you.
How can iron sharpen iron when you have no iron?

The honor is upon the minority, not the majority. I
can prove that through the life of Jesus. He wasn't
popular. We seek to be popular because we're insecure
and it exemplifies the nature of the enemy. He wanted
to be more popular than God. So, if that's in you, the
nature of the enemy is too. Truth is not popular.
Holiness is definitely not popular. Its religious jargon
used to sound appropriate. Anything you have to speak
to announce, you usually are not. God is tired of people
writing books and talking about topics they can't
demonstrate with their lives. If you can't demonstrate a
topic, you shouldn't teach/preach it. There was an era
where everyone was talking about minstrels. Everyone
is not a minstrel. Are you moving the crowd or the
cloud? When you're singing, something has to happen.
Worship is a mirror ministry. Worship shows you
about you, not the person standing next to you. Anyone
walking around during worship saying their discerning
things about someone else is a liar. During pure
worship, God's showing you yourself. The smokescreen
of you discerning everyone else's issues during
worship keeps you from seeing yourself.

Prophets, if you can't worship God and participate
in worship, you shouldn't be prophesying. You are
prophesying out of your gift and a familiar place. His
Word clearly states He is seeking someone to worship
Him- not prophesy to everyone (John 4:23). As a

prophet myself, clearly, I'm not against prophets prophesying, but you must learn you are subject to the worshiper expediting. Your title doesn't trump who is expediting at the time. In the apostolic church, I've often run into prophets that didn't want to yield to the minstrel who is prophesying through worship. If you can't honor God with your worship, how can you speak for Him? That's equivalent to you separating yourself from the rest of the Body, but God is not the author of confusion. Hold your hot prophetic word until after we worship the King. That's out of order and your heart is wrong if you cannot yield to what God is doing in corporate worship. This communicates that you have no respect for the ranking of the minstrel (and any other gift that God uses at will). That's out of order. Essentially most of the churches that have that order, look like a scene out of Prophets Gone Wild. That is rude and obnoxious, and God doesn't operate like that. When you dishonor those He's using and exalt yourself higher than them, you disrespect and embarrass them openly. If they can't handle me getting off the keyboard and snatching the microphone out of their hand- telling them, "That ain't it," what makes them think a minstrel can handle that and function well, after that. A title doesn't allow you to treat people like that. You deserve to be stopped, checked, rebuked, and put back in line. If we are supposed to be kings and vessels, you can't treat a king any kind of way. Why do we allow this to happen in the Kingdom? Jesus said He is the King of Kings. He was speaking of the kings that we are in His kingdom, with Him as the highest King. Historically, if you disrespect a king like that, you'll get your head cut off.

David was a warrior because he was ruthless. He knew the Kingdom's enemy and was going to handle the threats to the Kingdom. If we were more Kingdom minded, we wouldn't be fighting for a position. There are only so many positions, anyway. The frequencies that God gave me to tap into, keep the flow of God's blessings in the house. When I told leaders to stop dishonoring me, because they were dishonoring the flow of God's blessings, they laughed in my face. People can argue with your opinion, but they cannot argue with results. You don't have to prove anything to anyone. Just be who you are, and keep it moving. Being unafraid will hit the kingdom of darkness in the jugular.

Reforming our Community

In Chicago alone, on one street, for miles, there are 600 churches. All those churches are on different frequencies. On those same streets, there are liquor stores, drug addicts, and drug dealers. All these houses of rebellion refuse to link up to battle the same enemy, because they want the credit, alone. The songs your church is singing is keeping the old nature around. The songs are business as usual. There is nothing new coming out of their mouth. You have the same services with the same 10 people and leave and go home. You go to your lavish homes because you can't live in the communities you are not affecting. You want people to live there, but you won't. You can't even come together to evangelize one block. If the community reaches those people, all your churches will be filled.

We operate like the Illuminati. We don't want to affect our popularity. Don't you realize that you lost your reputation when you got saved? No one likes you. Get over yourself. You are not producing what God wants you to produce. When you go in a Church and they're still singing songs from the 80s and 90s, that's the enemy. When people come into your Church from being in the world after 15-20 years of being away, and hear the same songs they heard before they left-they won't stay long. The world's music will call them back after they've cried and got $10 from you. They've grown bored. We aren't singing songs that spark a new nature. Backsliders feel they haven't missed anything because you aren't doing and singing anything new. God requires us to do better.

We talk about traditional churches and denominations (that have regimented functions) like they are dinosaurs, but we're just as bad. We don't have enough love to display a more excellent way that lines up with the Word of God. We treat other denominations like they are less than us. To be "Pure [in] religion and undefiled before God and the Father is this, to visit the fatherless and widows in their affliction, and to keep himself unspotted from the world (James 1:27). That's the Word.

DAVIDIC REFORMATION

Chapter Ten
Results of Being Dishonored

I had an incident occur at a birthday party, where when I walked into the party the wife of the honoree asked me for one of my CDs. Knowing that a recording artist was booked to provide the music already, I shared that I didn't want to dishonor the artist by bringing out my music. However, the artist heard this individual complimenting and honoring me. After the event, I walked up to the artist to greet him and share what God gave me to share with him. He abruptly dismissed me saying, "If you wanna get with me, you go to my website." He was really nasty and missed a prophetic Word. He was intimidated by the attention I got while he was there. I'm sharing these things to show you the dishonor that can attack one's life and how unnecessary it is.

As a result of dishonor, it has taken me 25 years to accomplish something that should've only taken 25 days. I've had to promote my music on my own. I've had to take time to show people I was not a renegade like they were told by others. I was rejected because of my strong sense of identity, from systems that refused to identify me. I'm not bitter, I'm better. Saulic systems accuse people of bitterness because of their refusal of endorsement. I found that my lack of endorsement from a Saul system was actually my protection because the system could not contaminate me. So, I removed myself from the equation and contamination, and it saved my life. I had to realize the system was fighting me for something I was never after in the first place. I never wanted their endorsement. I saw the contamination of the system. Why would I want to be endorsed by a contaminated system I was sent to combat? You cannot change the system when the system is still in you. So I had to retreat and go get the system out of me. In the course of finding who I was, I discovered the grace of Jehu. When I went into places, I played in the purity of God's heart and found that it ruffled the feathers of Jezebel. She was denied access because I provided a pure environment. Jezebel cannot dwell in an atmosphere that is pure. In the process, I took it personally. God had to show me it wasn't personal and they weren't rejecting me; they were rejecting Him. Let me warn you. When you are a general or ambassador for change, you will face great accusation. Yet, you must know that if God sent you, He's also going to back you. If He didn't send you, you're in trouble. This should cause you to rejoice. When you have resistance, it solidifies you are in the perfect will of God. If you don't see opposition, it's a clue you are in the Saul system of people's choice. Being in God's will, will always bring you to the crossroad of "Do I want to be popular or effective?" You can't have both. When they lie on you, keep it moving. Stay focused. Your adversary is a sign to show you are on the same path. I tell the enemy, "You carry out your set of instructions, and I'm going to carry out mine." We serve the same God.

I learned from accountability vessels in my life, you don't have to respond to people unless what you are aspiring to is still in you. They aren't coming after your ministry. You don't have one. Your ministry is to serve and obey. You can tell if people are in a Saul or David system today if you get on Facebook. If they're in a Saul system their posts will brag about their church and pastor- not noticing they are not fulfilling their purpose. Most churches in Saul system are buddy systems. "Our pastor told us not to listen to you because..." (insert senseless reasons). They are bamboozled by the Saul system.

As an apostle, I'm not impressed by numbers when you've not done the work to get them. Numbers are deceptive. We discredit the church that has 12 people and label them ineffective. Yet, we don't know if the leader with 12 people went out to get those 12 and are building them up so they can go out and join the 12,000. You with the big church, you're usually evil, but no one wants to expose you- but God will. You lure people through the use of gimmicks. You lure Judah with more money, not relationship. You have stolen other leader's members and ask that same leader to speak at your church. How humiliating is that? You scandalize other leader's names and lure their faithful people when they can't see it. Again, I'm not impressed by numbers, if you got them the wrong way. There are plenty members to go around if we hit the streets. Instead, we trade members like baseball cards. Disclaimer: If this is not you, you have no need to respond. If it is you, you have the option to just repent and get on track. But know this, no weapon formed against me and people like me will prosper. I will continue to write, nevertheless. It's important for me to speak truth in this area because it affects me and people like me.

I said it before, Judah is the most used function in the Body of Christ, but the most neglected. Dishonor has developed into attempted murder, to kill their influence and effectiveness. More people have died from dishonor and a broken heart than disease- which is what follows dishonor. The things leaders have done to Judah; they would never allow to happen to them. From a ministering standpoint, that's why Judah is so greatly abused. Dishonor destroys the minstrel and psalmists' soul. Judah needs to be healed and delivered in her soul. The soul is where hurts, disrespect, and betrayal are suppressed for seasons. It's been ignored because the Saul system teaches you not to challenge leaders. Yet, that's not Biblical, because prophets came to challenge and correct leaders. Saul's system refuses to place honor on what God honors but has no problem honoring what's popular or someone who doesn't challenge them to do what's right. You're forbidden to disagree. The most detrimental action from Saul-influenced leaders is the release of labels out of their mouths. I shared with you earlier how I was labeled "rebellious" because I would not allow myself to be controlled, and labeled "renegade" because I did not agree with everything I saw and experienced. The deception in leader's labels is that they think the Word doesn't apply to them. They justify their actions with, "Touch not my anointed; do my prophet no harm." The Saul system and spirit is rooted in jealousy and murder. If the system cannot murder you physically, it will murder you spiritually and influentially. The characteristics need to be exposed because it always wants you to think the problem is you and not them.

The characteristics of someone with a Saul spirit are that he/she dangles promotion like a carrot to a horse, to keep you around. This spirit mimics God. They make promises, but the difference is they don't intend to keep theirs. I bind the spirit of "I'm gonna…" Another characteristic is they have no intention of honoring you if you don't do what they want you to do. Usually, think they have keen discernment. When they discern something of value in someone, they act like they have to ration out their influence concerning you. They become jealous of you. They possess layers of deception. The spirit of Saul can always see your inadequacies- never theirs. They even know the name of all of your demons, while theirs remain anonymous. That's a result of them not being involved in true worship because true worship shows you about you- not everybody else.

The Lord told me the problem with our worship is we have more critics than participants. Leaders are critiquing more than getting involved. They justify it by stating that they are busy measuring where you are, spiritually. Excuse me? Who ordained you to measure the worship when you are supposed to be participating? You won't get involved because your spirit will never allow you to recognize who is before you. Saul didn't even recognize David and that he was sent to help him. The cousin to this spirit is Anti-Christ. The same thing they did to Jesus; they did to David. They rejected Jesus when He came on the scene. Davidic order points you to Jesus.

We've become so deceived. We challenge anything that comes to correct us by justifying that what is being seen is not truly what is being seen. Some leaders have become the best illusionist. The Saul spirit produces the fruit of the cartel and dope dealers. In fact, that's exactly what the Saul system looks like. The mentality is, "I will only give you enough honor or product to keep you coming back to me." That's a dope-dealer spirit. "I'm going to control you because if I give you too much honor, you can supersede me and I can't let that happen." If you are a true apostolic father, your sons and daughters should supersede you. Jesus even said, "Whoever believed in me will do the works I have been doing, and they will do even greater works than these because I am going to the Father" (John 14:12). How can I do greater works in the Saul system when I can't get a merit badge for being faithful?

Healing from Dishonor

The best way to experience healing from dishonor is to first admit that you need to be healed. Every change has to begin with repentance. You have to repent for the involvement you had in the Saul system and how it made you feel. That's the best place to start. Some people will think, "I didn't do anything." My response is you need to repent for thinking you don't need to repent. We are guilty by association for remaining in a Saul system. We allow ourselves to stay in a place where we acknowledge a man's endorsement more than God's endorsement. We get caught up in what they dangle in our face. The leader dangles that Scooby snack in our face and we stay. This is also known as ordination, or as we see it in apostolic or prophetic houses, elevation. We are as bad as those we talk about. At least they have an honor system. I'm learning that most people who bash titles are people who don't have the capacity to honor people for who they are. I've had people personally call me "brother" to see how I would respond to being dishonored. You have to be confident in who you are. If God called you something and you've discovered it, you have to be confident in what He called you. You cannot be confident in what people recognize you as. You don't have to waste your oil or time on a fool.

God's honor system is important because how else can we look like him? In order for reform to have any validity, all parties involved need to search their hearts. There's no one person that's solely guilty. We are all one Body- not parts. When we are divided, we are in ruins. We've thought Judah was so insignificant that we are finding some leaders are dying prematurely because they've rejected what was sent to preserve them. Praise and worship was sent to the Earth to preserve your natural body.

We have made praise and worship user-friendly for us. We haven't sought God about the purpose for it. We don't release people because we think they were sent for us. We think dishonoring them and not releasing them will control them and keep them from being exposed to others needing what they bring to the Earth. One of the signs you're a controller is that you say, "After I poured into them and did this and that, they still wanted to leave." They are supposed to be sent and released anyway. Let them go! If you allow people to flourish in their respective areas, you'll have a relationship with them as if they never left. You'll always be attached and they will always remain loyal. We're only upset about releasing people because we won't evangelize to get more people into the Kingdom.

Leadership Excuses

Most of the decisions made concerning the music department are often instigated by the stockholders in the ministry. The people who navigate what goes on and doesn't go on are usually those who give the most in offerings and tithes. Because of the spirit of greed, leaders allow those type of people to dictate to them how they do or don't obey God. That's the real fruit of the Saul system. As a result, you pick songs that cater to the people, so that you can be their Saul (which is the people's choice). The theme song for that is, "Got to give the people, people what they want." The goal behind that is to please those who are supporting your livelihood. It forces divided loyalties on both sides. On the leadership side, you're torn between your obedience to God and faithfulness to man. On the congregation's side, they are torn between their loyalty to you and their faithfulness to God. So, the Saul system causes those types of conflict in the lives of the leaders and the congregation. Both sides are motivated by two different things.

Most leaders are motivated by their fear of losing people. So, they put the music department in a quandary by making them sing songs that are the favorite of the stockholders- but they are not favorites of God. I often hear leaders talk about what their people don't like. Honestly, who cares what your people like? What about what God is requiring? I often have said; the Bible is not a menu. It's not something to order what you like and reject what you don't. When it comes to music, the Lord said sing unto Him a new song (Psalms 33:3, 96:1). That settles it with me.

Chapter Eleven
Solutions for Leaders

Everything that sparks change has to begin with repentance. People need leaders to help them get healed. The anointing should flow from the head down, and so should deliverance. In some cases, deliverance should take place in the open, instead of some back room. This will influence people's faith. If you adopt the role of a father, you should openly show your children you're willing to do what you want them to do. They should be able to respond by saying, "I only do what I see my father do." However, they don't see you during worship. They don't see you until you make your grand entrance (after the worship). The only reason you don't participate is you think the worship is for you. We have the attitude that says, "The praise team has to make it conducive for me to preach." That's why we pick our own songs, so that we can speak- not for God to speak. If we worship God, most times, He will disrupt our plans. How can we give God a certain amount of time to do what He needs to? The Saul system is always time-conscious because it's worried what the people think. Our churches need to stop deploying and collecting the best of the best talent. We do not need auditions; we need interviews. We don't need ability; we need humility. We need to stop looking for music directors who have no relationship with God, and no relationship with you. We wonder why we see a high turnaround. They are not there to help you build or God build anything. They are there for a job. What we don't want to admit is the monsters that they become is because of something we've created. We won't challenge them to live right because we don't want to lose them. We keep enough flesh around to keep flesh around because our goal is to keep numbers high. That's why we recruit the best of the best. This needs to stop and we need to raise up those who understand covenant. Here's the deception: Most men of God are looking for schemes to get people to their church. However, Jesus said, "If I be lifted up, I will draw all men to myself (2 Chronicles 7:14)" Reformation has to be sought. We want people because we count them as tithes and offerings.

I have a serious problem with leaders recruiting celebrities and excusing them, because of the zeros behind their name. While, someone who has been with you for 20 years and faithfully building with you, is not given access to you. When it comes to the celebrity, it doesn't matter what they did the night before, they can come into your pulpit and preach. Yet, someone who has been with you for 20 years can't teach a Sunday School lesson. That's greed; but we label it as, "They need to be proven." You have been guarding your pulpit from everybody else, but you let celebrities in it. I've seen homeless people come into the church, and they are treated like they have the bubonic plague. However, people with a title that have orgies, criminal records, and sex-tapes can get in the pulpit.

What needs to be done is we have to stop being afraid of sitting people down that are ruining the church, but because they have talent so you won't stop them. Leaders are going through the women, but because they can also draw crowds to your church, you allow them to continue. We are afraid to confront this. We allow pimps to come and rape the church. They fleece the church and raise thousands of dollars, but the person that can actually bring the presence of God, you won't give them $20 to get home. We can't have gatherings or conferences unless we have a celebrity. They are used in the place where Jesus is supposed to occupy. When you create an environment where Jesus is the invited guest, He honors that. This is why Jesus doesn't come to many of our services because He is no longer invited. You have more people coming and leaving the same way. Only, they are broker, because they gave you all their money. The only thing that has changed is their bank account balance.

When Judah is cleaned up we begin to hear on God's frequency. We start getting His results- not our own. We are not following what God has told us to do. We are not simply following Bible. We give meetings according to our needs. I believe the Lord is requiring for us to meet the needs of others- as this is the purpose of ministry in the first place. David leveled the playing field, to ensure everyone was able to get what they needed in the presence of the Lord. We all need His glory.

If we are still getting the results we got in the world, something is wrong. People should not come to the house of God and still continue to deal with issues they dealt with in the world. They also shouldn't see the same things they are running from. They run to the church for help. They don't expect the same sins to be perpetuated. Backbiting, lying, treachery, and manipulation/control are yet being perpetuated in the church.

Dealing with the Music Department

Your overall music department should not be headed by someone more administrative than Spirit-filled. Administrators don't usually have the sensitivity to deal with spiritual things. There needs to be balance. I've seen ineffective setups. I've seen a worship pastor over the music department, but they usually are not knowledgeable about the technical side (microphones, systems, or sound quality). I've seen an elder over the music department who acts as a watchdog, but they aren't sensitive to the needs of Judah. You can't support anything you don't understand. When it comes to purchasing equipment, unqualified people tend to get the cheapest product available, because they're worried about the budget. This mindset is not concerned about the efficacy of Judah. That's why you'll see mega-churches with Casio keyboards on the platform. My problem is you won't spend enough money to ensure the music sounds correct and pleasing to God, but you'll bring someone in to entertain you and pay them top dollar. The priorities are off. I've been with leaders who brought in a famous celebrity and purchased extra equipment to make the guest sound better. Yet, the weeks prior, we were playing on cheap technology. The King of Kings and Lord of Lords should be the one we prepare for and seek to impress. Yet, we do all this to impress celebrities.

The music department is taken for granted. We don't even put honor on what Judah had to go through to get the sound right for corporate worship services. Let me interject this: sound technicians need to go through deliverance. They should be required to live a sold out lifestyle, and prepare themselves as if they are delivering a message in worship. It is important that their lives operate in purity to create a climate conducive for the Spirit to move how He wants to move. When the sound is off, it distorts the sound and the message being relayed. In times past, the sound technician gives what they think is needed, not what's being asked for. They play the role of God in our churches. If they worked for a celebrity with this behavior, they would be fired on the spot. I've seen sound technicians try to talk in technical jargon, to make you think you're stupid. There is nothing technical about, "Turn the sound up, step away from the board, and stop making adjustments." I've seen sound technicians who manipulate their control over sound. On occasions, I've been forced to bring my own sound system and still had them turn my sound down. That's demonic. That's the spirit of sabotage that Judah contends with. You only hear yourself through your monitor, because they're smart enough to turn you up in the monitor, but turn you down in the house speaker. The enemy takes away your effectiveness when your mic is turned down and muffled. This counteracts against the intensity of what's being released. Singers are better able to stay on key because they can hear themselves in the mic and make any modifications to support the authenticity of the sound God desires to release through them. We were instructed to worship with our gifts and He handles the crowd. It is not Judah's responsibility to worry about the crowd. Yet, the support of Spirit-filled and Spirit-led sound technicians help to produce the sound He requires.

You can't tell me that the pastor's mic is the only functioning piece of equipment. In many houses, they don't even show up until after the praise and worship are over. In the past, after the elder has opened service in prayer on the good microphone, I've taken the pastor's microphone. I knew the sound would be set perfectly on that mic. If you have more than one worship team in your church, I've had experiences where the sound technician has sabotaged the teams that were not his or her favorite. The favorite team's microphones and sound are superb and they have all the technician's support. This has to change.

Appoint People Appropriately

Only appointing people who agree with everything you say is evil. The person you appoint should be appointed based on their qualifications- not whether you like them or not. Nothing is wrong with someone who challenges you, as long as the challenge is in line with the Word, as opposed to being one's personal opinion.

As far as appointing musicians; there should be more emphasis on character and lifestyle than talent. There should be some form of diversity when dealing with transfer growth and new converts. You cannot use the same system to determine where transfer growth is, based on new converts. New members class is not for everyone. That's why you should have more interviews, than auditions-across the board. As I mentioned before, interviews help you learn the intentions of the heart. Auditions only allow you to go as far as the talent and what you discern about that, alone.

Trust God in People

We have to trust God in the people we appoint and respect their jurisdiction. If you appointed them based on the intent of their heart, it should not be difficult to trust their heart and their intentions if they were trustworthy enough to appoint. The lack of trust surfaces when you don't trust the people you put in place. It forces you to control them. You don't trust the God in them. Judah has a reputation of being untrustworthy, so you appoint people you can control. When you do that you restrict them from hearing God. They can't obey God when they have to obey you.

Stop acting surprised when you hire someone to do something and they do just what you hired them to do. The bottom line is, if you want a musician, you hire a musician. Don't be upset when they don't act like a minstrel. A musician does what is agreed upon in exchange for that check. The minstrel comes to assist and co-labor with you. They are usually covenantal people. What you give them, monetarily, is to bestow honor on them- not to maintain an obligation. A musician exchanges money for a service they provide.

There is a difference. If you, as the leader, agree to it, there is no reason for you to complain about it later. They are doing what they were hired to do.

Build Accountability

When strengthening your music department, Judah should not be separated from the rest of the auxiliaries and the congregation. The training they receive should not be treated like a Sunday School lesson. All parties should be held accountable. Currently, the music department is held responsible for the worship in our corporate settings. This is not the case in the intercessory ministry. The intercessors aren't the only ones praying. They lead the prayer and display the example. The music department has a responsibility to uphold, and so does the congregation. There should be a demand placed on both parties involved. The praise team shouldn't learn how to worship if the congregation or other ministry gifts don't worship. The whole Body needs to place a demand on the worship and hold one another responsible for it, corporately.

We are currently worshipping with people we don't know. You don't know people you see on Sunday. You don't understand who they really are. The person you get to know on Monday isn't the same person who shows up on Sunday. Anybody can get ready for game day and put on their game face. It's important that all auxiliaries have a relationship with one another, to kill the competitive spirit. I've seen scenarios where the prophets think they're better than minstrels. I've seen where the minstrels don't have a relationship with the prophets because they think they're better. There is conflict all the time. The only one they respect is the pastor. I've seen where none of the leaders have respect for Judah because they don't understand that Judah isn't made up of novices. Judah is not a novice to spiritual things. Just because they don't have titles does not mean they don't know spiritual things. You may have a title, but it doesn't mean you understand spiritual things. There will always be conflict when you're meddling outside of your jurisdiction. A prophet should not tell an intercessor how to pray. An intercessor should not tell a minstrel what to play. You're out of your jurisdiction. Yet, for some reason, all the auxiliaries feel they can tell Judah what to do and how to operate- even though it's outside of their jurisdiction. They don't understand the minstrel was not created to accommodate them, but to play and entertain the King of Kings and Lord of Lords.

Other Suggestions for Leaders

As we draw to the close of this book, I want to touch on some brief and final suggestions that will help facilitate healing and begin the process of cleaning up

Judah, until you can bring in a specialist to initiate reform. Have some type of intercession on a regular basis for Judah. It is a huge responsibility to be responsible for the spiritual climate in corporate worship. You have to first live in that climate yourself before you can create it in a corporate setting.

Create opportunities for Judah to be ministered to. We bring people in for everything else. You should always bring in individuals who have the heart to impart and demonstrate what they teach.

I pray that your eyes and heart have been opened to hear God's clarion call to initiate Davidic reformation in your corporate Body and individual life. Seek the Lord concerning what your next steps should be. If I can ever serve you or your house of worship to establish reform, do not hesitate to contact me. I long for the Body of Christ to return to the heart of the King and allow Him to release His sound throughout the Earth. Rise up, Judah!

DAVIDIC REFORMATION

About the Author

Jacques C. Cook is a prophetic minstrel in the purist sense of the word. Apostle Cook has ministered nationwide preaching, teaching, and releasing the sounds of Heaven. He currently trains minstrels and psalmists, teaching them the biblical blueprint of Davidic Worship.

Throughout his professional music career, he has written songs and composed music for billboard chart topping artists. He has written songs for Donna Summers, Faith Evans, Missy Elliot, and more, as well as composed music for commercials. He has ministered throughout the country, and internationally, in Mexico, Malaysia, St. Lucia and St. Kitts in the Caribbean, and Curacao in the Netherland Antilles, activating psalmists and minstrels to play prophetically.

Above Only Music Group originated and continues to expand through the gifts and leadership of this dynamic duo. They have dedicated their lives to help the least, lost, and forgotten. As a team, they work to impact lives in forgotten communities, through the love of Christ and by penetrating regions through the Arts and Community Development. They feed families, provide clothing and school uniforms for children, and repair/rehab homes for widows and U.S. Veterans. As often as possible, they provide free concerts and events for low-income communities.

For more information, visit http://aboveonlymusicgrp.org.

CPSIA information can be obtained
at www.ICGtesting.com
Printed in the USA
LVHW081531280319
612183LV00026B/350/P